AUSTRALIAN & NEW ZEALAND
CAKE DECORATING

AUSTRALIAN & NEW ZEALAND
CAKE DECORATING

Marie Sykes & Patricia Simmons

CHILD & HENRY
Sydney Australia

I wish to thank my husband Ken for his practical help and his patience over the years. Without his encouragement and assistance I would never have been able to pursue cake decorating as ardently as I have.

MARIE SYKES

First published 1981 by
Child & Henry Publishing Pty Ltd
27 King Road, Hornsby, NSW, Australia, 2077
© Copyright Patricia Simmons and Marie Sykes, 1981
Third Impression June 1982

Designed by Judy Hungerford
Edited by Sue Wagner
Printed by FEP International Pte Ltd
348 Jalan Boon Lay, Singapore
Typeset by Savage & Company

National Library of Australia Card Number and
ISBN 0 86777 112 7

JACKET PHOTOGRAPH

Three-tier wedding cake is decorated with Dorothy Perkins roses painted red and tiny pink gypsophila; it is finished with simple embroidery and a fine extension border.

The square blue cake features an assortment of Australian wildflowers including Christmas bells, wattle, flannel flowers, Sturt's desert pea, boronia and Christmas bush, trimmed with tiny moulded gumnuts and gumleaves.

The round yellow cake has piped flowers including daisies, pansies, snowdrops on wire, and fern, arranged around a flooded horseshoe.

In the foreground is a selection of moulded flowers.

Jacket photograph by Norman Nicholls

Photographs by Norman Nicholls, Charles Stoker, Eric Day, Ron Robertson

Three-tier wedding cake of clover shape, with formal roses and buds, white hyacinths and jasmine, pearl embroidery, extension work and lace. The clear plastic pillars were specially made for the occasion.

CONTENTS

INTRODUCTION

This book is a comprehensive guide to cake decorating. Through it we aim to help and encourage interested students to develop their own skills and craftsmanship. Use it as a reference book; you will find you achieve personal satisfaction as you become more proficient in this form of self-expression.

Repeated requests from students over the last decade have prompted us to make a more formal record of the various methods and techniques we use for decorated cakes, together with widely tested recipes and a few basic rules which do not change. Through the text you will find emphasis on the importance of correct consistency—of royal icing, covering fondant and modelling fondant particularly. As you gain experience you will find this easier to gauge. But attention to accurate measurement, careful sifting of pure icing sugar and thorough mixing are the vital points; they are noted in the recipes. Excessively hot or humid weather (not infrequent in our part of the world) can affect consistency—and again ways of dealing with this are covered.

Photographs of a selection of cake designs enable you either to copy the illustrated designs or to use them as a source of ideas for your own creations. But don't be too swayed by other people's work. Try to be original and develop your own style—and don't be afraid to experiment. Follow the basic rules and practise some of the main techniques—then self-expression can take over. Success comes with practice; if at first you don't succeed, try again.

Sugar flowers have been patterned and moulded from nature as far as practicable; however the natural colours have occasionally been toned to suit particular decorating purposes. We have included the most popular flowers, but have concentrated mainly on flowers which are not illustrated elsewhere. Australian wildflowers, our special feature, include many varieties that are new to decorators. Their vibrant colours will give wide scope and are especially suitable for men's and boy's cakes and special occasion cakes.

It is impossible to record every variation or theme in any one book, but we hope to stimulate your enthusiasm and develop your latent artistic ability to create a work of art in sugar.

1
EQUIPMENT

Piping Tubes

Ten basic tubes and two screws are required for the beginner. Australian brands readily available are Candyman, Ice Master and Durcher. The tubes are: *writing* 00, 0, 1, 2, 3; *star or shell* 5 and 8; *petal* 20 (small, medium or large; left-handed people must use a left-handed petal tube); *leaf* 16; *basket* 22. Additional tubes and screws may be added later as required. Test each tube with the screws to see that they move freely.

Icing Bags

Triangular icing bags, made from a rubber-lined material known as Jaconette, are available ready made from health food stores, or the material is sold by the metre in manchester departments of most large stores. Buy .25 metre and cut into four rectangles 44 cm x 22 cm (17½ x 8¾ in). To make up, fold cornerwise (rubber side in) and sew the side seam twice for extra strength, using a medium stitch. Attach the screw to a tube, then turn the bag rubber side out and push the screw and attached tube (screw end first) into the corner of the bag as far as it will go. Wind several rounds of strong cotton around the bag in the groove of the screw and cut off excess fabric with care; turn rubber side in to use. The folded edge of the bag must make a straight line with the attached tube, otherwise piping can be thrown out of line. Bags should be rinsed in cold water after use, turned inside-out and dried over a bottle. Keep away from strong sunlight.

Paper Icing Bags

Bags made of good-quality greaseproof paper are hygienic and useful for small areas of piping. Cut a rectangle 25 x 20 cm (10 x 8 in) (Fig 1), then cut it in half diagonally, for two bags. Hold the paper at D (Fig 2) and curve corner A to corner C (Fig 3). Take corner B around the cone twice to meet A. Tuck B into cone, or secure with adhesive tape. There should be a sharp point on the cone. Cut off enough of the tip of the cone to allow a metal tube, when inserted, to protrude about one-third of its length.

Put a small amount of royal icing into the bag with a knife, fold top of bag over and fold in firmly.

These bags can also be used for piping without a tube. Snip off a small amount of the point; for leaves, snip away each side to make a V.

Equipment

Medium peak royal icing and piping bag ready for filling

1
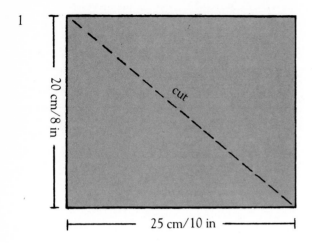

20 cm/8 in

cut

25 cm/10 in

2
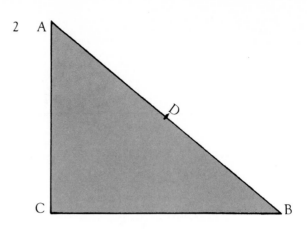

A

D

C

B

3
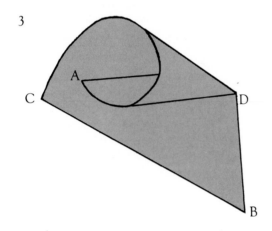

A

C

D

B

4
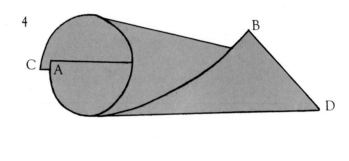

C

A

B

D

5
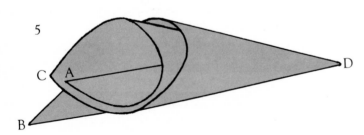

C

A

D

B

6
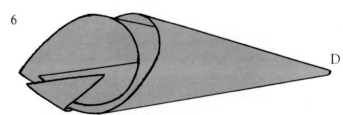

D

TO MAKE A PAPER ICING BAG

Cutters

Special cutters are available for different-sized petals such as frangipani, poinsettia and fuchsia, as well as rose leaves. Using cutters takes away the guesswork for beginners. As experience is gained some decorators prefer to model petals or leaves by the freehand method, while others recommend using cutters for certain flowers. An economical way to make your own cutters is by cutting strips of 12 mm (½ inch) .005 shim brass shaped and joined with solder or adhesive tape. Patterns are given on page 86.

Icing Nails

These are used for making piped flowers. They may be purchased ready for use at health food stores or made for a fraction of the cost by buying crown seal bottle tops, removing the cork, and glueing (with epoxy resin) or soldering flat-head nails to the underside. Piped flowers are quick, easy and colourful—but require practice. See photo page 61.

Scissors

Buy a pair of fine-pointed scissors and keep them for cutting small flowers, trimming petals or leaves and ribbon *only*. Buy the best quality; with care they will last many years. A second pair of cheaper scissors is necessary for cutting wire and paper.

Tweezers

Fine tweezers with long points are used when arranging delicate flowers and sprays, etc, as there is less likelihood of breakage.

Sieve

Specialist kitchen stores sell fine mesh bronze sieves. They are not expensive, and with care, will last a long time. Wash the sieve in cold water, wipe dry, and store in an airy place. When sieving icing sugar use fingertips only, not hard metal objects. If icing sugar is hard or lumpy, roll it out first and then sieve.

Mixing Bowls

Glass, china or plastic bowl (medium size) for mixing royal icing. (Metal discolours the icing.)

Wooden Spoons

Several wooden spoons, one of which is new and kept only for mixing royal icing. This is essential as even the smallest amount of grease will affect the consistency of the icing.

Stamens

Stamens are obtainable in many colours from most department and health food stores. Yellow, green and white are basic colours; the latter may be tinted as desired.

Turntable

A turntable is essential as the decorator progresses.

Colours

Vegetable dyes are used exclusively in cake decorating; they contain no harmful ingredients and may be purchased from health food stores. Cochineal is not recommended. Buy good quality dyes which are stronger in tone and last longer. Recommended colours for the beginner are: red, leaf-green, yellow, sky blue, brown, scarlet, apricot, rose pink, burgundy and mauve. Other colours may be added as required.

Non-toxic pastels (a type of chalk) are sometimes used to highlight various colours. Scrape the stick gently with a sharp knife, catching the powder in a saucer, and apply with a soft brush.

Storage of colours: An egg carton is handy to store the small bottles of colours as a safeguard against spillage. Turn carton upside-down and cut holes to fit bottle necks in each egg compartment. Position bottles, close the carton and secure each end with a rubber band. Mark the colours clearly on the outside of the carton and use them by just removing the bottle lids.

Colour blending is essential to cake icing and colour schemes should be well planned before commencing to decorate. Too many colours should be avoided. Pastel colours generally are more appealing to the eye and it is wise to use vivid colours sparingly. Test the colour first in a small quantity before mixing the full amount.

Consult the colour chart and try to visualize the many interesting colour combinations that can be made from the three basic colours: *red, blue* and *yellow*; red and yellow mixed in different proportions make salmon pink, orange, peach or apricot; red and blue make purple or violet; brown is obtained by using parisienne essence; blue and yellow make green. As there is a wide choice of commercially blended colours available it is much easier to buy them ready for use.

Two-tone autumn leaves are made by placing green and brown icing side-by-side in the same bag—the leaves will come out variegated. Several colours may be used together in the same way for multi-toned flower petals.

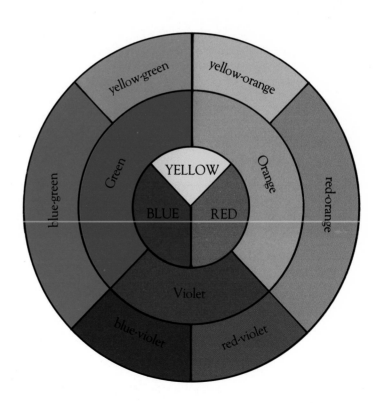

COLOUR CHART

Baby's bib and motif flooded in nursery designs.

Acetic Acid

Several drops of acetic acid added to royal icing help it to set firmly. It is usually stored with the food colours and may be purchased at health food stores.

Non-toxic Enamels

Greetings and names on cakes are often accentuated by the use of gold or silver non-toxic enamel to match the paper which covers the board. Enamel is obtained from newsagents, toy or hobby shops.

Crimpers

Crimpers are used to press designs into the covering fondant, mainly around the sides of the cake. Again, practice is the key word. A simple way to regulate space of imprint is to place a rubber band about 25 mm (1 in) from the open end. There are a number of different crimper shapes on the market.

Other Equipment

1 sheet heavy plastic used to cover the table or bench

Pointed end of a Size 2 (No 14) plastic knitting needle (for use in modelling flowers)

Wooden meat skewer; cut off half, and round the cut end with sandpaper

1 plastic spike (used for holding hair rollers in place with small round knob at one end, the other end rounded) used in modelling flowers

1 piece dowel rod about 20 cm (8 in) long for rolling modelling fondant

1 long wooden rolling pin, preferably about 70 cm (28 in)

2 or 3 good-quality artist's brushes (sizes 00, 1, 2 or 3)

Maize cornflour is used to dust fingers when modelling (Note that some "cornflour" is made from wheat; it is coarser and will damage fine petals.)

Plastic airtight containers or glass jars with screw-tops

Waxed and greaseproof paper

25 cm (10 in) masonite board or cake tin (for practising piping)

Large hat pin (useful for marking designs and many other things)

Dressmaking pins with coloured heads

Adhesive tape

Plastic ruler for measuring

Cotton-covered wire (fine, medium and heavy)

Sharp-pointed knife, penknife, craft knife or scalpel

2 pastry brushes (1 for egg white, 1 for paste)

Patty tins with rounded bottoms (for storing flowers and petals)

Good quality paper paste (e.g., Perkins)

Foam sponge cloth

Foil for setting flowers

Soft brush for dusting cake and board

Moulds for Easter eggs

Pillars for tiered cakes; wooden skewers (from butchers)

Note: Apart from the obvious household items, health food stores often stock decorating equipment.

Christening cake: a plaque flooded with nursery motif; piped nursery designs on the side, and border of simple stars with alternate drop loops.

2
ROYAL ICING

Royal icing can be used in a number of ways, for piping, for covering cakes (English style), for flooding or run-in work and for pastillage (both piping and moulding).

English decorators cover their cakes with royal icing, using two or three coatings at 24-hour intervals, smoothing each addition carefully with a wide spatula. As royal icing sets very hard, Australian decorators prefer a covering of rolled fondant, with glucose added to keep it soft and smooth. However, the addition of four to five drops of glycerine for every egg white will keep royal icing firm on the outside, while soft underneath and easy to cut. Glycerine is not used in royal icing for general pipe work.

Royal icing is probably the most important icing you will have to make, so take time to mix it well.

Royal Icing Recipe
1 egg white at room temperature
250 grams (8 oz) pure icing sugar, sieved through a fine mesh
   bronze sieve (do not use a flour sieve)
¼ teaspoon liquid glucose *(optional)*
2 or 3 drops acetic acid

Beat the egg white lightly in a glass bowl with a new wooden spoon absolutely free from grease. Add sieved icing sugar, one tablespoon at a time, beating well after each addition. For fine extension work, a small amount of glucose added to the royal icing gives a smoother texture. Finally add the acetic acid.

This process should take about 20 minutes; there is no shortcut to beating, as air has to be beaten *through* the mixture, not into it. When ready for use the icing should be light and smooth; it will form and hold a smooth peak on the spoon when pulled away from the mixture. This consistency, known as **medium-peak**, is suitable for most piping. **Soft-peak** icing, used for embroidery, requires a little less icing sugar—the peak should gently drop to one side. **Firm-peak** icing requires an extra teaspoon of pure icing sugar to a tablespoon of medium-peak royal icing. Firm-peak icing is used for piped flowers and in the assembly of moulded flowers.

Transfer the mixture to an airtight container, or cover the basin with a damp cloth if using immediately, otherwise a crust will form and block up piping tubes. Well-made royal icing will keep for several days and still be suitable for fine work if correctly stored. However, the icing does need further beating before use if it has been left to stand.

For the quantities given, use a 55 gram (2 oz) egg. Larger or smaller eggs yield different amounts and as experience is gained you will be able to judge quantity to suit your requirements.

Pure icing sugar only is used. Icing mixture includes a little cornflour to keep it soft. For that reason it does not give the correct consistency. If in doubt, test by placing 1 teaspoon of the icing sugar in half a glass of water. Stir until dissolved. If the liquid is clear the icing sugar is pure; if cloudy, it is icing mixture and not suitable for our purpose.

Sugar granulates quickly and crystallization commences after several days, so it is necessary to sieve carefully, making sure not one grain of sugar slips through the sieve. If in doubt as to the fineness of the mesh, sieve the icing sugar again through a piece of muslin or a clean nylon stocking.

PIPING TECHNIQUES

To Fill the Bag
There is a correct way to fill an icing bag; it is also the easiest way. Screw the tube on to the bag and place the bag over a small glass, folding it back over the glass to leave a cavity for the icing (see photograph). Place a table-spoon of royal icing in the cavity; use a knife for easier handling. Do not overfill the bag.

To Hold the Bag
Grasp the twisted end of the bag firmly between the thumb and forefinger; close fingers around the bag and squeeze gently; guide the tube with the free hand. Paper bags are held in the same way, with the thumb on folded end of bag. First, learn to control the icing, to pipe evenly, and to start and stop as desired. The amount of pressure and steadiness of hand determines the size and uniformity of design. Some decorations require very little pressure, e.g., embroidery, which is done with soft-peak icing, generally using a fairly fine tube. Correct pressure is learned by practice. Cleanliness is essential when piping. Have a damp cloth handy to wipe off excess icing and always commence to pipe with a clean tube. Right-handed people work from left to right, while left-handed people work in the opposite direction, except for writing and printing.

Two-tier wedding cake with single roses, lily of the valley embroidery, extension work and simple lace.

The bag must be held at the correct angle. There are two basic positions: 90° angle and 45° angle to the surface. When piping stars and dots, the bag is held perpendicular (90° angle); when writing and embroidering, it is held at a slant of 45° to the surface.

Start with one of the larger writing tubes (size 1 or 2) for the following exercises.

Writing Tubes

Dots and pulled dots; snail's trail

Dots: Place the point of the tube (at 90° angle) against the surface, squeeze gently, stop, then lift the tube away. Dots should be round and smooth, without a point; they can be made in varying sizes, depending on the amount of pressure exerted. Five dots in a small circle with a centre dot form a forget-me-not. Forget-me-nots bloom in various shades of blue, but when decorating they can be coloured in any desired shade to complement the colour scheme.

Pulled dots: As for dots; squeeze, then lift the tube gently away so icing forms a small vertical point.

Teardrops and Snail's trail: Pipe a series of pulled dots (holding the bag at 45°) in a teardrop shape, each bulb covering the tail of the previous teardrop. Snail's trails are often used to neaten the cut (bottom) edge of fondant covering on cakes, around the base of bridgework and to outline a design or plaque.

Herringbone; scrolls; hollyhocks

Herringbone: Holding bag at a 45° angle, pipe teardrop shapes alternately from left and right. This too can be used at the base of fondant coverings.

Scroll: Pipe the letter "C" (at 45°) and then below it a reverse "C", joined to the tail of the previous one. Scroll-type decorations are used on edges, sides and bases of cakes.

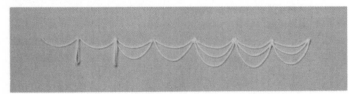

Dropped loops

Loops: Loops are used as a side border decoration, piped at a 90° angle. Touch the tube to the side of the cake, squeeze gently, then take the tube away from the surface, allowing the loop to fall naturally in a gentle curve. Until you have experience it is wise to measure and lightly mark the distance between loops to ensure an even design.

Lattice: Place the tube on the surface at 45°, squeeze gently

Lattice

and raise the hand slightly to control the direction of the icing thread. Squeeze gently (*do not pull* as this will break the thread), then ease pressure and touch down to the cake. If the thread is allowed to touch the cake while being drawn across it will result in a crooked or broken line.

Hollyhocks: Pipe a thread resembling a stem (at 45°); then, commencing from the bottom of the stem, pipe a small circle and over-pipe the circle about three times to form a small cone. When dry, finish with a small yellow pulled dot in the centre. Pipe about four to six blossoms grading from large at the base to small at the top. Hollyhocks can be piped to blend with colour, style and design variations.

Swan and reeds; rabbit

Swan and Reeds: This is an attractive decoration used mainly on Christening cakes. Pipe the tail at a 45° angle in four neat strokes slanting upwards; lift the tube and make a figure 2 for the head and neck; continue in an anti-clockwise movement to fill in the body; finish with three heavy-pressure strokes (towards the tail) for the wings. On the head, pipe a large dot pulled downwards to form the beak. Reeds are piped as a thin downward stroke, thickening near the top with heavy pressure and a slight zigzag movement, then relaxing to a fine stroke.

Rabbit: The rabbit is simple to pipe: a dot for the head, a larger dot for the body, two upward strokes for ears and a small white dot on the body for the tail. They can be piped in grey, white or brown.

Bird in a tree; chickens

Top tier of a wedding cake has a bride's slipper filled with Cecil
Brunner roses, blossoms, hyacinths and forget-me-nots.

Bird in a Tree: Pipe branches to resemble a tree and sit a bird on the branch: make a large pulled dot for the body, with tail pulled up to the right; pipe a smaller dot for the head, and a pulled dot for the beak, slanting upwards towards the left. The wing is piped into the body as another pulled dot.

Chicken: A chicken is piped in the same way as the bird (without branches), with the addition of two legs and claws. Colour the icing yellow and touch up the legs and claws after they are dry with brown colouring.

Cornelli: Cornelli is a simple rounded movement piped at 45° as a random all-over pattern. There is no visible start or finish; the design is not angular or separated. Cornelli makes a spectacular side or top pattern design, but it must be done neatly to look effective. Use one of the smaller writing tubes and soft-peak icing for the best results.

Grapes; cornelli

Grapes, piped with No 2 tube and firm-peak icing, make an attractive decoration; they may be piped directly onto the cake (at 45°), or piped on waxed paper, allowed to dry, and then placed on the cake. They can be green, deep burgundy or variegated colours. Pipe a solid pear-shaped base and allow it to dry. Turn the point to the top and commence piping at the point, simple teardrops, building them up to resemble a bunch of grapes. Allow to dry. Tendrils may be added using a No 00 or 0 tube; leaves are piped with No 16 or 17 tube.

Star Tubes No 5 and 8

Stars; shells; shell border

Stars: Stars are piped at a 90° angle, the movement being: press, stop, remove. Size depends on pressure exerted; a large star requires heavy pressure; a small star, light pressure. They must touch one another when piped around the base of a cake.

Variations are produced with the aid of a writing pipe. For a base, pipe around the cut edge with stars lightly touching, then pipe smaller stars in the spaces just above the first row. Change to No 0 or 1 writing tube and pipe a line from the centre of a small star to the centre of the nearest large star, then back to the centre of the next small star in a zigzag pattern, until the round has been completed. If desired, work between alternate large and small stars to form a diamond pattern.

Another variation of the single star border is to drop shallow loops between the points of alternate stars; then move to the next star and repeat.

Scrolls piped with star tubes

Shell border: Hold the bag at 45° with the tube lightly touching the icing; squeeze heavily, at the same time lifting the bag just off the icing, then gradually relaxing pressure while bringing icing to a point or tail. The next shell is piped over the tail of the previous one. Shells are used mainly for borders at the base of a cake. Other variations such as fleur-de-lis, reverse shell, scrolls, herringbone, etc, are done holding the bag at the same angle.

Dancing lady borders; star border with dropped loops

Dancing lady border: Commence piping from the base upward, making a shell, but this time pull the tail up to a long point, 25 mm (1 in) or more; repeat all around the cake, each point being the same height, and with no space along the base between shells. Then change to No 0 or 1 writing tube and pipe a series of gentle curves between alternate points around the cake, and another series between the other set of alternate points. Finish each point with a small dot.

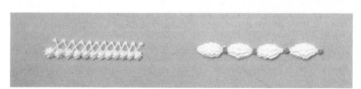

Double star border with crossed threads; puff border

Puff border: Holding the bag at 45° angle, touch the tube to the surface; use alternately light pressure and heavy pressure, at the same time moving the tube in a gentle zigzag movement to form the puff border. It can be piped with two colours in the bag or over-piped with No 1 tube, to make drop loops between the narrow points, or tiny piped flowers or large contrasting dots at the narrow points.

Fleurs-de-lis; cradle weave

Cradle weave: This is piped in the same way as basket weave (page 20), using No 5 star tube.

Leaf Tubes No 16 and 17

Leaves: Use firm-peak icing and bag held at a 45° angle. Leaves may be piped directly onto the cake or onto waxed

Three-tier hexagonal wedding cake with white gardenias,
snowflakes and small forget-me-nots. Scattered embroidery is simple,
in keeping with the edging of scallops. The top tier has a bride
and groom placed in front of a curved shape which is piped.

paper. Another way is to place wire on waxed paper and pipe a leaf over and along the wire; when dry, peel the waxed paper off. Pressure is: squeeze hard, then ease and lift. If the leaf is not sufficiently pointed, pinch the tip gently between thumb and first finger. Leaves can look attractive if piped with two or three colours side by side in the bag.

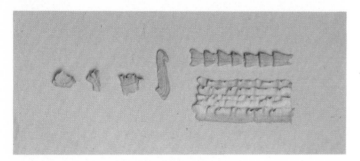

Leaves (various types); frills; border (leaf pipe)

Frills: Leaf tubes may also be used in making single-sided or double frills. For a single-sided frill, hold the tube on its side on the surface of the work. For a double frill, hold the tube at a 45° angle, squeeze hard while moving steadily across the surface.

Dolly Varden cakes: These may have frills and stars piped as an all-over design instead of fondant covering; use four to five drops of glycerine to every egg white to keep the royal icing soft.

Petal Tube No 20

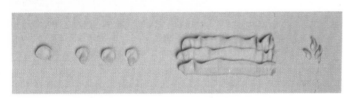

Basic petal; frill using petal tube; wisteria petal

To pipe a petal: Hold the tube at a 45° angle, concave shape facing toward you and the short end pointing upwards; make a horseshoe movement, keeping the tip of the tube close to the work.

Dolls with piped skirts: Dolls are attractive ornaments on children's or debutantes' cakes and it is more interesting to pipe a skirt than to practise on a board. Dolls are shown in three sizes: 50 mm, 75 mm and 100 mm (2 in, 3 in and 4 in). Try the largest size first as they are easier to handle. Cut a skirt in light cardboard to fit the doll; fix it firmly around the doll's waist and down the back seam with adhesive tape. Hold the doll by its head, upside down. Commence piping petals around the bottom of the skirt. The next and subsequent petals are piped just beside and slightly overlapping the previous one. When the first round is complete, start the next round just above, in alter-

Dolls with piped skirts

nate spaces, working in rows towards the waist. Then change to No 5 star tube and pipe bodice with tiny stars. Sprinkle edible glitter (see page 72) lightly on the dress if desired. **Note:** Ordinary glitter is *not* edible.

Ribbon Tube No 22

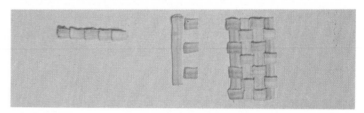

Basket weave

Basket weave: Holding bag at a 45° angle, practise basket weave on a tin first, making sure the weave is straight and even by lifting the icing from the surface when piping. Follow the step-by-step photos. When piping a basket weave cake, use four to five drops of glycerine for every egg white to keep the royal icing from becoming too hard.

Basket weave cakes may be made in different shapes. A square cake can have an open lid of cardboard, lined with silver or gold paper. The sides of the cake and sides and top of the lid are piped in basket weave. Moulded or piped flowers, or moulded fruits and vegetables, may be placed in the basket.

A large bow of ribbon adds to the finishing touch. Round cakes may be finished as a basket with a large handle and a large bow. The handle, made from wire, is covered with twisted fondant or ribbon. Other basket suggestions are: a strawberry basket, vanity case, sewing basket (containing genuine articles or ones moulded from almond paste or fondant and tinted), picnic basket, fishing basket and handyman's basket.

3
CAKE TINS AND CAKE COVERINGS

CAKE TINS

Sizes of Tins

Care should be taken when choosing the tin for your cake, as the shape and proportions of the finished cake are important. A small amount of mixture in a large tin will produce a flat cake that looks like a biscuit when decorated. Similarly a large amount of mixture in a small tin will produce a too-tall cake. Use a reliable recipe and be guided by tin sizes specified. Most standard recipes using 500 g (or 1 lb) butter and 500 g (or 1 lb) brown sugar will yield a 4.5 to 5 kg (10 lb) cake and will fit a 255 mm (10 in) tin.

For a three-tier cake the standard sizes of 250 mm (10 in), 200 mm (8 in) and 150 mm (6 in) look elegant and well balanced. For a smaller size, 230 mm (9 in), 180 mm (7 in) and 130 mm (5 in) are suitable; the recipe quantities should be adjusted accordingly.

Choose tins that are free from dents for a smooth finished cake with less packing to be done before decorating. Buy matching sets of tins for tiered cakes.

Preparation of Tins

Grease tin thoroughly, or spray with cooking spray. Use two thicknesses of greaseproof paper to line the tin (*not* waxed paper as it clings and is difficult to peel off when baked).

For a round, oval or heart-shaped tin, cut two pieces of greaseproof paper about 12 mm (½ in) larger in diameter than the base of the tin; cut a fringe about 12 mm (½ in) deep; spray or grease thoroughly and place on the bottom of the tin, smoothing over carefully. Spray or grease a folded strip of greaseproof paper and carefully smooth all around the sides of the tin (inside), making sure there are no ridges. (Do not use aluminium foil inside the tin as mixtures tend to creep under the foil during cooking.) Place foil, brown paper or newspaper around the outside of the tin (secured firmly with string) to prevent burning. *For a square or rectangular tin,* cut two strips of greaseproof paper, each the width of tin and long enough to cover base and two opposite sides. Spray or grease, then place them crosswise in tin. Cover outside of tin as for round tin.

PREPARATION OF BOARDS

Time and effort spent in decorating a cake will be wasted

Lining a tin; preparing a board (undersides of board shown)

if the cake is presented on an untidy or uneven board. A few extra minutes of preparation pay handsome dividends to the final presentation. Use Masonite or plywood, cut approximately 50 mm (2 in) wider than the uncovered cake, or slightly larger for bridge or extension work. You will eventually arrive at your own choice of size.

Four runners, strips of wood 6 mm (¼ in) wide, forming a smaller square underneath the board, are glued in place, so the weight is evenly distributed. They make handling of the cake easier.

Select a paper to cover the board; it should suit the colour scheme of your cake and be of harmonious design. A busy design tends to detract from the cake, so it is advisable to choose a simple unobtrusive pattern or plain coloured or gold or silver paper.

Cut the paper about 50 mm (2 in) larger than the board. Brush the top of the board all over with a good quality paper paste. Place the paper on the board and wipe over with a damp cloth, carefully smoothing out any air bubbles or excess paste. Turn the board over, brush paste to the edges of the paper and firm paper onto the board with a damp cloth. Allow board to dry completely before use. To protect the covering paper, brush centre of board with egg white, cover board with waxed paper, brush again with egg white, and centre cake on board. Use ruler to check that it is accurately positioned.

MARZIPAN OR ALMOND PASTE

Marzipan is made in three qualities: (a) from ground almonds, (b) from almond meal and (c) from marzipan meal. Ground almonds are simply almonds ground very finely, almond meal is a mixture of sweet and bitter almonds, while marzipan meal is ground peach kernels.

When almond meal is unobtainable try grinding the required amount of blanched almonds finely in a blender. An alternative would be to substitute 150 g (6 oz) rice flour or ground rice, with a few drops of almond essence to taste; however this does not have good keeping qualities. Coconut (sometimes recommended as a substitute) is inclined to go rancid after a short time.

Almond or marzipan paste is used mainly as an under-coating for rich fruit cakes, or for simnel cakes (popular at Easter time), for kidney potato cakes (small pieces of génoise cake covered with almond paste, moulded to resemble a potato and dusted with grated chocolate), and for petits fours.

Marzipan Recipe
750 g (1½ lb) pure icing sugar
125 g (4 oz) almond meal, ground almonds or marzipan meal
2 tablespoons sherry *or* orange juice
2 egg yolks
4 teaspoons lemon juice
1 teaspoon glycerine
2-3 drops almond essence (*optional*)

Sift icing sugar into a bowl, add almond meal and mix together. In a separate container place egg yolks, sherry (or orange juice), lemon juice and glycerine and beat with a fork to blend. Add to dry ingredients and mix to a smooth paste. If too dry add a little extra sherry or orange juice. Knead lightly until smooth, using a little sifted icing sugar. This quantity covers a 250 g (½ lb) cake.

Applying Marzipan to a Cake
Cakes sometimes need to be trimmed with a large sharp knife so that the top is uniform in height. When trimmed, turn the cake upside-down so that the bottom becomes the top, ensuring a smooth, level surface. Roll the marzipan into a smooth loaf shape and for a square cake divide into six pieces, four smaller pieces for the sides of the cake, one larger piece for the top and the end used for packing. Pack around the base of the cake if necessary and plug large holes made by the fruit.

Take one of the four side pieces, roll to size of a side of the cake, about 6 mm (¼ in) thick; trim to size. Brush marzipan with egg white, and place halfway along one side and around the corner, firming it onto the cake with the palm of the hand. Continue around the sides, making joins at the centre of each side as neat as possible.

Roll out the remaining marzipan for the top and use the tin in which the cake was baked as a cutter for the exact size. Brush the top of the cake with egg white and carefully place the marzipan in position. Run the rolling pin *lightly* over the top and smooth the joins carefully. It should now be smooth and even all over. Brush the cake over lightly with egg white. When dry, this forms a seal between marzipan and icing, preventing oils from

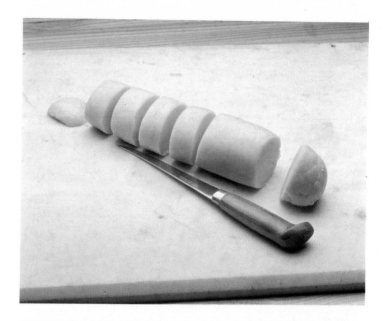

Marzipan cut, rolled, and applied to a cake

Child's birthday cake: decoration painted directly onto the cake. Trimmed with single roses, blossoms and brown boronia. Fine extension work and lace embroidery completes this prize-winning cake.

the cake seeping through to the fondant and discolouring it. This method can be adapted easily for shapes such as round, oval, six and eight-sided cakes.

COVERING FONDANT

Covering fondant is the finishing coat to your cake. A well covered cake is proof of a good decorator, so take time to do it well. Make it a rule always to cover your cake in daylight. Small hairline creases which are not seen under electric light become glaring imperfections in the bright light of day. Fondant covering handles well in moderate weather but during hot or humid weather it is wise to get up early and cover your cake while the temperature is low. The fondant covering will go on more easily and you will remain cool and calm.

Remember to sieve the icing sugar well, several times if necessary. The table or surface on which you are working must be clean and free from tiny lumps of icing sugar. Cleanliness and tidiness are essential.

For those who do not like marzipan, an extra coating of fondant will give a smooth finish.

Most decorators try different fondant recipes before settling on the one that suits them best. We suggest you try several, then make your choice. Our coverings (more recipes page 82) have been tested by students over many years and found to be reliable, provided all ingredients are weighed and measured accurately—this is most important. Always buy fresh ingredients (preferably from a busy supermarket) and check the date stamp. Sieve the pure icing sugar several times with a fine sieve (*not a flour sieve*—the coarse mesh allows grains of sugar into the mixture). Allow the mixture to cool, but not get cold. The mixture could ferment or the gelatine could be stringy if directions are not followed.

It is wise to make your covering fondant at least 24 hours before use and store it in a plastic bag. Gently knead into shape before use, taking care not to over-knead as this can cause air bubbles. Always colour icings in the daylight; artificial light is very deceiving.

Covering Fondant Recipe 1
1 tablespoon gelatine
60 ml (¼ cup) water
3 tablespoons liquid glucose
3 teaspoons glycerine
7 cups (approx. 1 kg/2 lb) pure icing sugar
Flavouring and colouring (optional)

Place water in a double enamel boiler (or heatproof glass bowl in a saucepan), add gelatine and stir over low heat until dissolved; *do not boil*. Remove from heat, add glucose and glycerine, stir until combined, and allow to become cool, but *not* cold. Carefully add the colouring at this stage, because it mixes more easily; add flavouring if required.

Place 5 cups sieved pure icing sugar in a basin; make a well in the centre. Add liquid and stir with a wooden spoon until the sugar is absorbed. Place into an airtight container and leave 24 hours; this helps to eliminate air bubbles. Then knead in the balance of the icing sugar until mixture feels satin-smooth. Cover and allow to rest for a further hour. Do not leave the fondant uncovered; if you are called away, place it in a plastic bag or an airtight container. This quantity will cover a 2 kg (5 lb) cake.

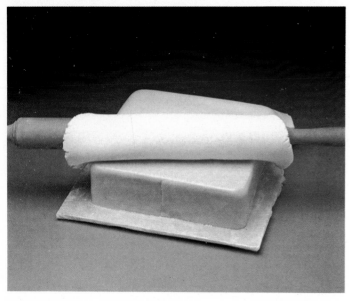

Applying covering fondant

Applying Covering Fondant
Clean table or work surface, then dust it lightly with sifted pure icing sugar. Place fondant on surface and use a long rolling pin (also dusted lightly with sifted pure icing sugar) to roll it out to about 10 mm (⅜ in) thick, large enough to cover top and sides of cake. Brush the cake with lightly beaten egg white (this adheres icing to cake). Drape fondant over rolling pin, then lift it carefully and centre it on the cake; take care not to stretch the fondant.

Use the palms of the hands (dusted with icing sugar) to smooth over the top of the cake and eliminate air bubbles. Work corners, cupping the hand, and the sides, using the palm of the hand. Work as quickly as possible, because fondant will begin to crust. Firm fondant into base and trim off excess with a knife held vertically.

Carefully remove any visible waxed paper from board.

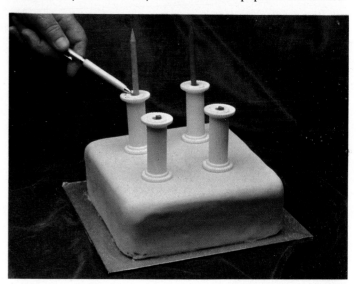

Pillars for tiered cakes

Pillars on Tiered Cakes
Pillars are used on tiered cakes to support the upper tiers. When buying pillars measure them side by side to make sure they are all of uniform height and the bases are level. Pillars are attached at least 24 hours after covering fondant was applied, and before commencing to decorate. Decorate each tier separately and pack them in individual cartons for transportation, then assemble at the destination.

Step 1: Cut a greaseproof paper pattern the exact measurement of the supporting cake. Mark on it with pencil the position of the pillars. A good guide is to have pillars in line with the corners of the cake above (not the board of second tier). Mark the cake by piercing the pattern with a needle or skewer.

Step 2: Remove the pattern and insert a skewer into each marked position, then reverse the skewer so the flat end of the skewer rests on the board of the supporting cake.

Step 3: Slip a pillar over each skewer; with a pencil mark the skewer in line with the top of the pillar.

Step 4: Remove pillars and skewers from cake, noting their individual positions. Cut each skewer at pencil mark. Replace into the cake in the same position as before. Take care that the skewers are not cut too short as this would cause the pillars to sink into the icing.

Step 5: Pipe a small dot of royal icing under each pillar to secure it to the covering fondant. Subsequent tiers are handled in the same way.

4
CRIMPER WORK, RIBBONS AND TULLE FANS

CRIMPER WORK

Crimper work is a simple form of decorating, which is imprinted with a special tool to give a serrated edge look. Large and small crimpers and many different patterns are available. The work is done mainly on the top edges and sides of cakes while the covering fondant is still soft. Once the imprint is made it cannot be erased, so practise on a spare piece of fondant before attempting to decorate a cake. Measure and mark with a pin or fine needle to keep the design level and even. Place a rubber band about 25 mm (1 in) above the serrated edges of the crimper to restrict the depth of the imprint, so patterns are easier to regulate. Dip the crimper tip into cornflour so the icing does not stick to it.

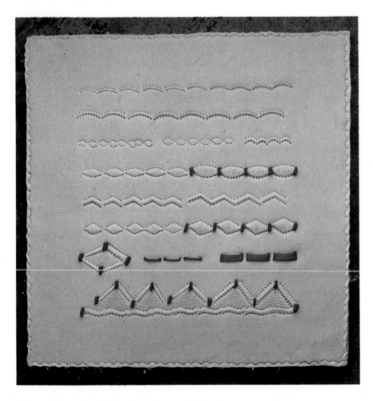

Crimper work; ribbon insertion and loops

RIBBON INSERTION AND 'THREADING'

These techniques can be used in combination with lace and embroidery or crimper work.

Insertion gives the illusion of ribbon looped through the covering fondant. This is also done while the fondant is soft. Choose or tint ribbons (see page 28) to match or contrast with the covering fondant.

Step 1: Cut the required number of pieces of ribbon 12 mm (½ in) long, and fold each in half.

Step 2: With a sharp pointed craft knife make a shallow incision in the covering fondant (do not cut to the almond paste), large enough to accommodate the ribbon. Using tweezers to hold the ribbon, carefully place the two raw edges into the slit in the fondant.

Threading: Cut narrow ribbon to required lengths (approx 25 mm/1 in). Fold ends in about 3 mm (⅛ in). Measure the exact distance between the folds and make shallow incisions in the soft covering fondant this distance apart. Insert ends of the ribbon into the slots. Leave a small space between pieces of ribbon.

RIBBON LOOPS

Loops of ribbon may be used as a decoration to add daintiness and colour to a spray of flowers, also as a camouflage

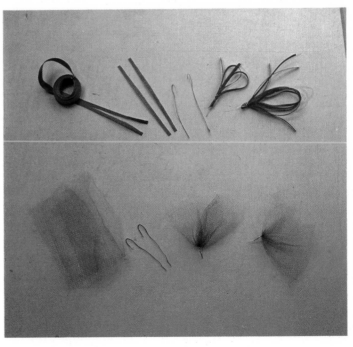

Tulle fans; ribbon loops

Plaque of wildflowers which includes waratah, flannel flowers,
Christmas bush, wattle, bottlebrush, cocky's tongue, running
postman, wild flax, native rose, cassia, gumnuts, eggs and bacon,
broom and tea tree.

for the back of flowers where petals are joined. Buy the narrowest ribbon. Cut it neatly in halves and remove frayed edges by pulling firmly through the thumb and forefinger; if very fine ribbon is required, cut off the selvedge and use it only. Ribbons are bunched in loops and secured by binding the ends firmly with fine wire, leaving small ends of wire to poke into the icing. Keep the ribbon ends as small and neat as possible.

RIBBON BANDS

Sometimes the design requires a ribbon band around the cake; this can be used in combination with extension work,

lace and embroidery, also to emphasize unusual shapes of cakes. Measure and cut ribbon and attach to cake 24 hours after applying fondant; secure ends with a pin and a spot of royal icing (remove pin when icing is dry).

TULLE FANS

These are used mainly to camouflage backs of flowers. Cut a small rectangular piece of tulle, fold firmly into pleats and secure at the centre with fine wire. Then fan one side of tulle to the left and one side to the right. Twist ends of wire together so this can be neatly inserted into the cake. Use fans sparingly and keep them small.

5
POPULAR MOULDED FLOWERS

Moulded flowers can be very fine, and realistic in colour and shape. Their possibilities are endless, and once you have controlled the techniques you will enjoy creating your own. Practice is the keyword.

Modelling Fondant Recipe
2 teaspoons gelatine
1 teaspoon liquid glucose
30 ml (1 oz) cold water
160 g (5 oz) pure icing sugar
Extra sifted icing sugar

Place water in a double enamel boiler (or heatproof glass bowl in a saucepan), add gelatine and stir over low heat until dissolved; *do not boil*; add glucose and stir till dissolved; allow to cool slightly, but not to become cold. Add 160 g (5 oz) sifted icing sugar a little at a time, stirring until it is absorbed. Leave for 24 hours in an airtight container at room temperature to set.

When ready to commence modelling, take a spoonful of the mixture and gradually knead extra sifted icing sugar into it until it has a consistency similar to plasticine and is no longer sticky. We have found this method, adding the balance of the pure icing sugar just prior to modelling, most satisfactory as the modelling fondant keeps better for a longer period. Place in a plastic bag and allow to rest for a few minutes.

Remember to keep modelling fondant covered at all times and to store it in an airtight container, but not in the refrigerator.

MODELLING TECHNIQUES
Freehand modelling
This is the main method for petals. First dust the fingers lightly with maize cornflour. Roll a small piece of modelling fondant to a teardrop shape, squeeze to flatten it, then work with a gentle squeezing, stroking movement of the thumb and forefinger around the top edge till it is as fine as possible. Tips of petals can be fingered so finely they are almost transparent; they may then be delicately curved or fluted. This takes practice; however it is well worth the effort. Don't allow fondant and cornflour to build up on your fingers. Keep a damp cloth handy to wipe them, then re-dust with maize cornflour.

Cutter method
Special cutters are available in a wide variety of shapes which enable leaves or petals to be cut in one movement. This is faster than freehand modelling — a skill which requires many hours of practice. It's worth trying both methods, however, for the various flower shapes, before deciding which you prefer, or for which flowers. Most experienced decorators use cutters for frangipani.

When using any type of cutter, stamp out the required number of petals for a flower from one piece of fondant and cover them with a lid or glass to prevent drying. Finger the edges of each petal to take away the cut look. Then assemble as required for the particular flower.

When making leaves, give them a slight twist or a lift do not dry them flat.

Shaping petals
Petals are shaped by pressing the cushion of the finger or thumb into the petal which is resting on the palm of the hand. The petal is curved from tip to base.

Veining
These light marks along the edge of a petal are achieved by rolling a ridged implement lightly over the petal. A ball-end spike, or a paintbrush or skewer with a slight ridge is suitable.

Stretching, fluting and ruffling
To *stretch a petal*, place the edge along the forefinger and roll a knitting needle firmly but gently along the edge. If the veining implement is used in place of the needle, veining and stretching are completed in the one movement.

To *flute a petal*, place the petal along the forefinger and roll knitting needle or skewer very firmly along the edge, then use point of knitting needle to gently ripple the edge.

Ruffling is done in a similar way for larger petals, producing deeper ripples. Place the petal on the palm of the hand, with base of petal pointing towards the wrist. It may seem awkward at first, but a little practice will make it second nature.

Shapes used for drying
Certain petals need to be held in shape while they dry.

A *cardboard cylinder* (from inside a roll of plastic or waxed paper) cut in halves lengthwise is an excellent shape for setting sepals and long petals.

A *cardboard cone*, built up with modelling fondant like

a large rosebud, makes an ideal shape for setting the throat of the *Cattleya* orchid with the desired curve. (A cardboard cone is also used as a base for piping Christmas trees.)

Round-bottomed patty tins are used to dry and store rounded petals, holding them in a lightly curved shape.

A *foil ring* is used to give shape to the outer row of gardenia, carnation and camellia petals. The gentle curve gives the flower a fuller appearance. Shape a strip of kitchen foil into a ring about 2.5 cm (1 in) across and 6 mm (¼ in) deep. Cut a 9 cm (3½ in) square of foil and mould it over the ring, flattening the centre. Petals are placed around the circle, with their points neatly meeting in the centre, allowing their edges to curve over the ring and rest on the foil.

Colouring

There are several methods for moulded flowers and decorations:
a) Fondant can be coloured before modelling.
b) Petals can be painted when dry, before assembling.
c) Fondant can be just tinted an appropriate paler shade of the finished colour; this makes them easier to paint afterwards, specially for bright or dark colours.

Stamens and wires may be tinted by dipping them briefly into a small amount of methylated spirits to which a few drops of food colouring have been added. Place on a tissue and pat dry.

White rayon ribbon should be dipped first in clear methylated spirits, then colouring added to the spirit and the ribbon dipped again. Quickly wipe the full length of the ribbon with a tissue to absorb surplus moisture and avoid spotting.

WORKING FROM NATURE

When you have mastered the main techniques for moulded flowers, you will enjoy devising your own, working from nature. SELECT TWO CHOICE SPECIMENS. Keep one in water for reference, for assembly and colouring. Turn the other upside-down; carefully remove the back row of petals and lay them in the same order on a sheet of paper. Trace around each petal, or, if petals are all the same shape, trace one and note the number in the row. Mark the tracing to show the petal base. Repeat if necessary for subsequent rows of petals. Label or number for easy recognition. Note colour, size and approximate number of stamens. Note shape of calyx. Cut patterns in light cardboard. Make a sample flower while the reference bloom is still fresh, colour and store your sample for future reference.

FORMAL ROSE

The formal rose, a popular freehand moulded flower for all types of cakes, may be used by itself or combined with other flowers. This rose has about 11 petals which open out from a tight bud centre. First colour the modelling fondant to the desired shade. The base (centre of the flower) is made by the flag method.

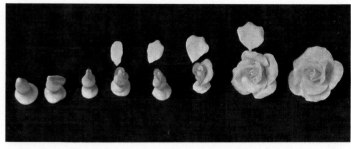

Formal rose

Step 1: Take a ball of fondant about the size of a 10-cent piece, bring the top to a point and press a waist into the centre, leaving the balance to fan out and form a stand. Place the stand on a firm surface. The top forms the bud; its size determines the size of the finished flower.

Step 2: Dust the forefinger and thumb lightly with cornflour and gently squeeze from the pointed top, down one-third of the bud, to form a small flag. Using a paintbrush moistened with water or egg white, brush the flag and wrap it around the tip to give a spiral effect. This is now the tight bud, the centre of the rose.

Step 3: The next petal is small and wraps about one-third of the way around the bud; secure it and all other petals at the base with a spot of water or egg white. Mould two more petals slightly larger in size and attach. The fourth petal begins to open on one side. It and subsequent petals are made in a teardrop shape, fingered out as finely as possible on the top edges. Press over the forefinger to give shape and attach each petal overlapping the previous petal by about one-third until the desired shape is achieved.

Step 4: When the rose is complete, cut the base off carefully with a knife or scissors to make a neat finish. Set for at least 24 hours in a patty tin and store away from dust.

DOROTHY PERKINS ROSE

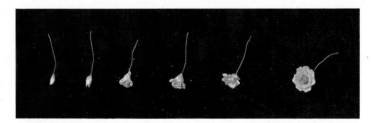

Dorothy Perkins rose

This is a tiny climbing rose which combines well with other flowers and adds a soft finish. They are moulded freehand and are about the size of a 5-cent or 10-cent piece when finished, the larger size being merely the addition of an extra row of petals. Their natural colour is pale pink, but decorators may use any colour to blend with their colour scheme. Cut and hook a supply of fine wires first.

Step 1: Take a very small piece of modelling fondant and make a bud using the flag method (above).

Step 2: Mould three tiny petals around the centre bud.

Two-tier oval wedding cake trimmed with pale apricot coloured open roses, brown boronia and hyacinths. Half-moon extension work, lace and embroidery, add the final touch to this elegant cake.

Step 3: Mould four or five petals with slightly curled back edges and attach to the bud.

Step 4: Mould another five petals with curled edges and attach them. If a larger size is required, add another row of five petals.

Mould a few tiny pointed buds on wire; when dry, paint a green calyx.

SINGLE ROSE

Dainty Bess and brier or wild roses may be modelled free-hand, or you may prefer to use cutters until you are familiar with the shape of petals.

Step 1: Roll out a piece of modelling fondant using a small length of dowel rod or a skewer. Select the desired petal cutter and stamp out five petals. Cover four petals while

Single rose and Christmas rose; rose hips

working on the fifth so there is less likelihood of their drying and cracking. Finger the top edge of each to take away the cut look.

Step 2: Place a petal over the forefinger and brush the edges backwards to form a soft curve, then place petal in the palm of the hand and use the cushion of the fourth finger to gently cup the base of the petal into a curve. Make two more petals this way, with edges curving out.

Step 3: For the remaining two, which curve inward, place the petal in the palm and shape slightly by applying gentle pressure with the cushion of the fourth finger. Place all five in shallow patty tins to dry for at least 24 hours.

Step 4: When dry, petals may be tinted if desired with diluted lemon or pink colouring, shading from darker at the base to a very pale colour at the tip. They may also be tinted on the back only, if desired.

Step 5: To assemble, use firm-peak icing and No 5 tube filled with royal icing in a matching shade or pale yellow. Take a 5 cm (2 in) square of waxed paper or foil and squeeze a small star of icing on the centre. Place one curved-back petal, then a curved-in petal on the royal icing; position the remaining petals, overlapping in spiral fashion. Pipe a very small star of royal icing in the centre and place the stamens around or completely covering the centre. (Be liberal with stamens, as they soften the appearance of the flower.) Left-over cottons from stamens may also be used for centres if they are dipped in colour, or dipped carefully (one at a time) into egg white and then into natural-coloured gelatine.

CHRISTMAS ROSE

Heleborus niger is not a true rose, but because it blooms at Christmas in the Northern Hemisphere it is called the Christmas Rose. As the delicate white and green colouring blends well with gaily coloured festive decorations, it is used extensively on Christmas wrappings and greeting cards, etc. The egg-shaped petals are cut in the same method as for single rose.

Step 1: Cut five petals and finger the top edges.

Step 2: Cup the petals as for single rose, but do not flute. Allow to dry.

Step 3: Paint the base of each petal lightly with pale leaf green.

Step 4: Assemble as for single rose, studding the centre liberally with creamy-gold stamens. This rose may be tinted pale pink instead of green if desired.

FULL-BLOWN ROSE

Full-blown rose

Full-blown roses are a favourite decoration, but there are many petals to be moulded, grading from large to small, and the stamens are arranged in a slightly different way from the single rose. Colour the fondant a pale shade of the final colour to make tinting easier.

Step 1: Select three cutters graded in size small, medium, and large and cut five petals of each size. Finger the cut edges and vein the petals. Large petals are shaped over the finger and curl outwards, medium petals stand up (cupped gently in the palm with cushion of the fourth finger), and the small petals curve inwards slightly.

Step 2: Secure a tight cluster of stamens with fine wire and tint them an apricot colour.

Step 3: To assemble, pipe a small circle of royal icing using No 5 tube and place the large petals in a spiral fashion, slightly overlapping each other.

Step 4: Pipe another small circle inside the first circle and add the row of medium petals.

Step 5: Add a little more royal icing in the centre, place the small cluster of stamens in it, then fill in with longer stamens until the royal icing centre is covered.

Step 6: Place the row of small petals in position between the stamens and the medium row of petals. There should be no royal icing visible.

SWEET PEAS

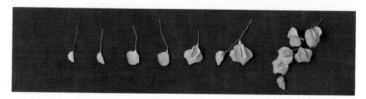

Sweet peas

Sweet peas bloom in reds, pinks, blues, mauves, yellow, cream and two-tone effects. They are moulded freehand and are a favourite with decorators.

Step 1: Mould a small crescent-shaped bud and insert a hooked or knotted wire. This is the basic pea foundation. Prepare sufficient in advance and allow to dry.

Step 2: Shape the keel or first petal and mould onto the base to completely cover it. At this stage, it can be used as a bud, with painted calyx.

Step 3: The two lateral or wing petals are moulded, pressed

*Three-tier wedding cake of scalloped oval shape, baked in
specially-made tins. It has tiny blossoms, white hyacinths, snowflakes
and forget-me-nots. Tiny moulded bells on the sides of the cake,
above them dainty sprays of flowers. This is a style for the
experienced decorator with plenty of time.*

out very finely, veined and attached with a spot of water on either side of the keel petal.

Step 4: The posterior or standard petal is rounded, softly fluted, veined and attached curling backwards. Add a little variation to each shape by twisting or curling the petals. Colouring may be added to the fondant or as a tint when the flower is completely dry. Use a darker colour for the inside petals and lighter for the standard petal. Make sprays using one or two buds and three or four flowers.

FIVE-PETALLED BLOSSOMS

Blossom

Many types of blossom which are similar in structure, and distinguished mainly by colour, such as cherry, apple, pear, peach and quince, may be made in this way. Colour may be added to modelling fondant or painted on the petals when they have set. Try painting the backs of petals different colours for variety.

Step 1: Cut five petals using one of the smaller cutters.

Step 2: Finger top edges carefully and vein if desired.

Step 3: Cup each petal in the palm, using the cushion of the fourth finger for shaping. Place in patty tins until set.

Step 4: To assemble, squeeze a small star of matching royal icing onto a square of waxed paper or foil; place the five petals in a circle, neatly overlapping at the base. Place at least twelve soft yellow stamens in the centre (more may be used to give a softer appearance). Allow to dry. Care must be taken when removing foil or waxed paper.

To lend height to the spray, mould several small five-sepal calyxes (as for Eriostemon — page 42) and secure each to the back of a dry blossom while the calyx is still soft. Then wire several blossoms together.

FRANGIPANI

Frangipani

Popular and extensively used, frangipani (also called *Plumeria*) are mostly white with yellow centres, but pale and dark pink varieties are also seen.

Step 1: Roll out a piece of modelling fondant. Using the frangipani cutter, cut five petals.

Step 2: Finger the edges and cover four petals with a glass.

Step 3: Place one petal in the palm of the hand and roll a paintbrush handle across the petal, pressing from left to right, to make the left-hand side curve inwards. Place on a board and brush a little water half-way up the right edge of the petal.

Step 4: Repeat for the second petal. Then place it on the board, overlapping the first petal by about one-third. Repeat for other three petals.

Step 5: Pick up all five petals with a small knife and fold the flower inwards so the fifth petal now falls behind the first, overlapping by one-third, to give a spiral effect in the centre. Squeeze the base of the flower gently and stand in a small narrow-necked bottle. Use a dry brush to open out the petals gently with a right-to-left movement, touching only the flat part of each petal. Allow to dry.

Step 6: When dry, paint with soft yellow, easing the colour off to white at petal tips. Pastel chalks also give a life-like glow, and are easy to apply.

The half-open flower is made in the same way, but not opened out with the brush. Calyx and wire may be added to some flowers to give elevation when arranging. Be sure wire is strong enough as flowers need support.

For buds, take a small piece of modelling fondant about 2 cm (¾ in) long and roll to a soft point. Make five slight incisions towards the base and give the bud a gentle twist. When dry, add a touch of diluted lemon or burgundy colour near the incisions.

FUCHSIA

Single fuchsia

Fuchsias vary in size from delicate miniatures to large double blooms and in colour from champagne to deep purple.

Single Fuchsia

Step 1: Group 7 or 8 stamens (including one longer stamen) and bind firmly with fine wire. Tint if desired.

Step 2: Wrap a tiny circle of coloured modelling fondant around the wire and allow to dry overnight. This is the base to which the petals will be attached, not part of the flower.

Step 3: Roll out a quantity of modelling fondant and stamp out four petals of suitable size with a cutter. Finger the edges and cup each petal lightly. Place petals side by side, overlapping slightly, and secure each with a spot of water.

Step 4: Lift the petals with a knife and place on the palm of the hand. Take the prepared stamens, lay them in the

Twenty-first birthday cake with frangipani, pale pink, mauve, and white blossoms, and snowflakes. Extension work has been piped on the rounded end, with a snail's trail and embroidery on the long shaft.

centre of the petals and wrap the petals around the stamens, making sure they overlap. This is the corolla. Finger the base to secure and leave to dry for 24 hours.

Step 5: Cut four sepals with the special cutter and finger the edges. Attach each one to the base of the dry corolla, firming and fingering them to form the tube (sepals and tube combine to form the calyx). The base of the calyx may have a tiny green ball (the ovary) added; this is optional. To dry, stand some flowers up in florist's clay, and hang others down, so you get a variety of petal and sepal shapes.

Special note: The drying periods specified are essential; in the long run they save time and lessen the likelihood of breakage.

Double Fuchsia

Double fuchsia

Double fuchsias may have as many as 36 to 40 petals which are curled, twisted and folded, with numerous tiny petals. As this would be impossible to mould in sugar, the following method will produce a realistic flower. Again colour choice is left to the decorator; there are many combinations, from champagne to the deepest reds and purples.

Step 1: Assemble the stamens as for single fuchsia.

Step 2: Cut 7, 8 or 9 petals with a cutter of suitable size, finger lightly, cupping some and curling others. Attach each to the centre with a spot of water, overlapping the petals. If curly petals are required they should be left for 24 hours to dry, then the remainder added.

Step 3: Cut and finger 4 or 5 tiny petals, curling and twisting each to give a realistic look. Attach them underneath the flower (not down the wire) and push them up close to the base petals to give fullness. Attach each with a spot of water and allow to dry.

Step 4: Add sepals by the same method as for Single Fuchsia.

LEAVES

Leaves form an important part of the colour balance in floral arrangements. There are many different types from which to choose; some of the most popular and spectacular are maple, holly, gum, lily, ivy, clover, shamrock and rose (see patterns page 86). Geranium, begonia and coleus leaves make ideal decorations for men's or boys' cakes where flowers are not desired.

Roll out a piece of modelling fondant. Rose leaves may be stamped out with a cutter; others are cut freehand or using cardboard patterns. For serrated edges, use a sharp knife, scalpel or razor blade to make tiny shallow cuts.

Mark centre vein, then smaller veins, with the back of a knife, taking care not to cut right through the leaf.

Twist each leaf slightly before drying to give a natural appearance. When dry, paint rose leaves with dark green colour and softly blend into the leaf a spot of yellow, brown or burgundy. Colour other leaves as desired.

ORCHIDS

Cymbidium

Cymbidium orchid

These orchids may be modelled in a range of hues from red, brown, orange-yellow, palest pink and mauve to yellow and white. (Watch colour balance with bright colours.) The *Cymbidium* consists of three large rounded sepals, two winged petals, a throat and a column; see patterns page 87. Tint the modelling fondant to an appropriate pastel shade or off-white; this makes the finished flower much easier to tint to the required shade.

Step 1: Cut out three sepals, finger edges and vein. Dry over a curved surface (see diagram).

Step 2: Cut two wing petals, finger edges, vein and dry across a curved surface, set in opposite positions to make a pair.

Step 3: Cut out the throat, finger and ruffle from points A to B. Set over a curved surface to match sepal (Step 1).

Step 4: Cut or shape the column and dry over a curved surface to correspond with sepal and throat. Tint petals as desired and allow to dry.

Step 5: To make up; use firm royal icing, a No 8 star tube and a square of foil or waxed paper. Set the three sepals into icing to form a triangle (at 12.00, 4.00 and 8.00 positions). Place the wing petals (left and right) into position (10.00 and 2.00). Push the throat into the royal icing, in centre. Place the column behind the throat. Pipe two small pollinia on the throat (each a small snails' trail) and colour them yellow.

Cattleya

Cattleya orchid

These orchids can be distinctive and elegant; they bloom in the palest of pinks, mauves, yellows and white. One or two combined with a few small flowers and ribbon

Two-tier octagonal cake with frangipani, delicate mauve bells and
white hyacinths; embossed rose embroidery on the sides, with
extension work, lace and bluebirds complete the picture.

loops can be very commanding. Do not spoil the effect by over-decorating. See pattern page 87.

Step 1: Cut two wing petals and finger cut edges. Drape each petal over the forefinger and press a fine knitting needle against the edges to flute (from points A to B). Vein each petal. Place lightly in a patty tin to dry.

Step 2: Cut three sepals, finger the edges and vein. Flatten the base and set to dry in a soft curve in a patty tin.

Step 3: Cut one throat. Finger edges, flute as for wing petals (from A to B) and set to dry on a cone built up with modelling fondant. (The column is made last, and set while soft into the dry throat.)

Step 4: Tint petals as desired before assembling: the throat is touched with yellow, diffusing to the main colour at the ruffled edge. When dry, make the column and set it into the throat. When column is dry, lightly touch the scalloped edge with apricot or light brown.

Step 5: To make up, pipe a star of firm royal icing on a piece of foil or waxed paper. Place the three sepals in 12.00, 4.00 and 8.00 positions. Add the two frilled petals and last the throat with column attached. Small pieces of cotton wool or crumpled waxed paper may be used to support the petals while they are drying. As you become more proficient you will find you use less royal icing in assembling. Orchids may also be set directly onto the cake if desired.

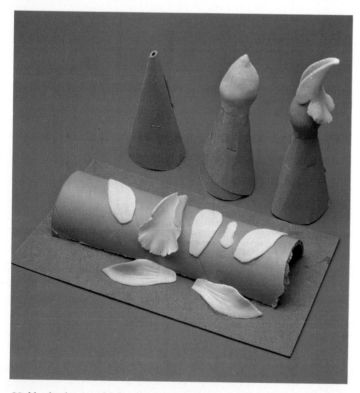

Half-cylinder mould for drying cymbidium petals; cone for drying cattleya throat

Phalaenopsis

Phalaenopsis (or moth orchid) is one of the most beautiful orchids. Brides often carry this flower and request a matching spray on their wedding cake. There are many varieties

Phalaenopsis

and colour combinations; our pattern (page 87) was made from an actual flower by taking it apart and tracing around the petals and various parts. It varies greatly in shape from the *Cattleya* and *Cymbidium*. The *Phalaenopsis* has three sepals, two wing petals and a throat; the throat has a front lip and two side lobes (made separately and attached) which curve gently towards the column; just below the column sit the pollinia.

Step 1: Cut three sepals, finger edges and vein lightly. Set them lightly in a patty pan; do not curve the sepals as this is a flat flower; pinch each tip gently, to a point.

Step 2: Cut two wing petals (1 left and 1 right), finger edges, vein and stretch the edges but do not flute. Set to dry in a patty tin with a *very* gentle curve.

Step 3: Cut one throat, finger edges, place on the palm and press lightly with cushion of finger so the whole piece curves gently upwards.

Step 4: The column, a tiny piece shaped like a hollowed-out comma, is curved over the forefinger and flattened at the base.

Step 5: Cut two lobes, small petal shapes (1 left, 1 right); vein lightly. Place in the palm and cup gently with the cushion of the finger.

Step 6: Shape the pollinia from a tiny oval piece of modelling fondant, indenting with a knife to resemble two pieces side by side. Trim the back to enable it to sit flat. Allow all pieces to dry thoroughly.

Step 7: With creamy-yellow paint, tint across the centre of the throat, the pollinia and the lower half of each lobe (back and front); allow to dry. Using a very fine brush and diluted burgundy colouring (not red), lightly paint veins on the lobes (above the yellow) and down the centre of the column (but not to the front lip). Paint a few minute dots on the pollinia. Allow to dry thoroughly. Paint a small spot of yellow-brown on the curved tip of the column.

Step 8: To assemble, pipe a small star (No 5 or 8 tube) in firm royal icing on a square of waxed paper or foil.

Step 9: Place the top sepal first, then left and right sepals (12.00, 4.00 and 8.00 positions).

Step 10: Place the left and right wing petals between the sepals (10.00 and 2.00).

Step 11: Place the base end of the throat into the icing, then add the column at the base of the two wing petals, forming a curve from the top of the column to the lip of the throat.

*Two-tier oval wedding cake: sweet peas are featured on this cake
with miniature daisies; piped birds in the embroidery on the sides
of the cake, together with extension work.*

Step 12: Place the pollinia on the throat, between the two pointed side pieces.

Step 13: Place the lobes on either side of the column, making sure the yellow part of each lobe is at the bottom and the burgundy streaks at the top.

Step 14: When thoroughly dry, if desired, pipe two fine whiskers on the end of the lip, one on either side.

These flowers are very delicate, and can be handled more easily if wired. To wire, mould a five-petal calyx, insert hooked wire, and add the soft calyx to the dry flower. The flower can be placed face-down on cotton wool or tissues to allow the calyx to dry.

CARNATION, GARDENIA AND CAMELLIA

Camellias, gardenias and carnations all have the same basic method of construction, the main difference being the shape of the petals. Several of these flowers combined with a few sprays of small contrasting flowers make beautiful posies for many types of cakes.

Carnation

Carnation

Carnations bloom in many colours from white and pastels to deep vibrant shades and variegated colours.

Step 1: Using the carnation petal cutter, stamp out six petals. Finger cut edges and vein right to the edge of the petal, making it slightly ragged. Set petal points neatly touching within a foil ring (page 28) attaching them to each other with a spot of water. Outside edges rest on the foil.

Step 2: Cut six more petals, handle as Step 1, and set alternately with the first row. The petals stand up slightly.

Step 3: Cut another six petals, handle as Step 1, and set alternately with the second row; petals will stand up.

Step 4: For the centre, cut three petals, handle as Step 1, then pleat each in a concertina fashion. Put a spot of water on the base of each petal and insert one at a time, overlapping each other. Push them down gently to give a slightly crumpled look. Allow to dry.

Step 5: For the calyx, mould a 2.5 cm (1 in) green tube and hollow out with a knitting needle. Cut into five small pointed sepals in the top. Moisten top of tube with water and firm onto the dry carnation. Put flower face-down on cotton wool.

Step 6: To complete the calyx, mould a shallow five-pointed cup and finger the base to a short stem. Moisten the cup with water and attach to the end of the tube. Allow to dry.

Gardenia

Gardenia

The gardenia, a white flower with three rows each of six petals, has a centre composed of three small banana-shaped stamens in a yellow or mustard colouring when fully opened, or small, tightly-overlapped petals before the fully-open stage.

Step 1: Stamp out six petals using a rose petal cutter. Finger cut edges and bring the top of each petal to a shallow point. Use a little water to set petals in a circle, slightly overlapping, on a foil ring. This outer row of petals may be curled back slightly.

Step 2: Cut six more petals, handle as Step 1, and set alternately with the first row.

Step 3: As Step 1; set petals alternately with second row.

Step 4: For the 'bud' centre, cut three petals, handle as Step 1, and overlap them tightly into a pointed bud. Moisten the base and insert in centre of third row of petals.

Step 5: For the full-blown centre set three mustard-coloured stamens into the centre of the flower after Step 3.

For elevation in arranging, mould a five-petal calyx, insert wire and adhere with a spot of water to the dry flower.

Camellia

Camellia

Camellias bloom in shades of pink, white, red and variegated colours.

Step 1: Mould a solid teardrop-shaped centre (size depends on size of flower). Allow to dry.

Step 2: Cut three petals, finger cut edges and wrap them around the teardrop centre. Allow to dry.

Step 3: Using a small petal or frangipani cutter, stamp out seven or eight petals. Finger the cut edges and give the petals a gentle backward curve by placing them over the forefinger and stroking with the thumb. Place the petals in a circle, points meeting in centre of foil ring and edges overlapping slightly; moisten overlapping side edges of petals so they adhere to each other.

*Tiered wedding cake: full-blown roses with hyacinths and
snowflakes, horseshoe-shaped embroidery with embossed roses, and
extension work.*

Step 4: Cut another seven or eight petals, handle in the same way as Step 3 and place alternately with the first row.

Step 5: As Step 4; place petals alternately with the first row.

Step 6: Set the dry centre of the flower (Steps 1 and 2) into position. Place some flowers on wire, adding a five-sepal calyx, moistened with a spot of water to attach it.

TIGER LILY

Tiger lily

Tiger lilies bloom in shades of orange streaked and spotted with dark brown, deep pink with burgundy, white with yellow and many more. The spots of contrasting colour match the heavy stamen heads. Some types have petals curled back, others have petals just barely curled. Some have slightly fluted edges, others have straight edges.

Step 1: Stiffen seven long stamens by coating them with clear nail polish and attach triangular heads of modelling fondant to six of them (stamens); to the seventh (the stigma) attach a small green ball of fondant at the tip. Allow to dry, then colour stamens as desired.

Step 2: Cut six petals (pattern page 86), finger cut edges, vein, slightly flute and set to dry over a curved surface. Give some petals a slight twist.

Step 3: When the petals are dry, paint to the desired shade, with deeper colour towards base of petals.

Step 4: Using royal icing and No 000 tube, pipe tiny dots on each petal; allow to dry. Colour the spots to match the stamen heads.

Step 5: To assemble, push a square of waxed paper or foil into an egg cup. Squeeze a spot of royal icing into the centre of the square and set three petals at 12.00, 4.00 and 8.00 positions, the points meeting at the centre; then add the other three petals at 2.00, 6.00 and 10.00 positions.

Step 6: Push stamens and stigma into centre of royal icing; support if necessary with cotton wool until set.

DAISIES

Daisies

Daisies can be made in all colours from white or yellow with yellow centres to bright colours such as pink, red, blue or orange, with suitable coloured centres, for Cinerarias or Livingstone daisies. Colour centre yellow or as desired.

Step 1: Mould a dome-shaped centre 6 mm (¼ in) across. Insert prepared medium weight wire and allow to dry for at least 24 hours (see page 48).

Step 2: Shape a basic hollow cone (see page 41), cut in half, then cut each half into five equal parts.

Step 3: Working quickly, mitre each point about half-way down the petal, to a long slender shape.

Step 4: With knitting needle press each petal back gently against the forefinger, at the same time slightly grooving the petal. Give some petals a slight twist or an upward lift. Press each tip to a gentle point.

Step 5: Paint a spot of water at the base of the petals and pull the wired centre lightly through; firm it on. Cut off any surplus at back of flower, keeping this part as flat as possible.

For a double daisy add another row of 10 petals slightly larger than the first row, placing them in alternate positions just behind the first row.

6
SMALL MOULDED FLOWERS

Small moulded flowers, used with larger ones to form sprays, help give balance of colour and size. A selection of small flowers may be used in many colours. Requests are often made for dark or very bright colours; to preserve colour balance, you may wish to restrict the strongest colours to small flowers. Try some of these, then experiment with your own ideas. Concentrate on the correct shape first; size may be adjusted when proficiency is obtained. Remember, the smaller the flower, the smaller the piece of modelling fondant. Always dust fingers with cornflour before commencing to model.

Stamens
You will need small stamens, or the cottons left over from stamens for small flowers. They can be coloured to match or contrast with the flower. White, coloured or two-tone stamens can be purchased.

To colour stamens: First dip the heads into methylated spirits, then add the colour to the spirits, quickly dip the stamens again and spread them out to dry, patting with a tissue to remove surplus moisture.

To curl stamens: Place between the thumb and the blunt edge of scissors blade, and pull firmly through. Stamen cottons may be curled in the same way.

Wires
Some small flowers are wired so that they can be arranged in clusters or made into a spray including several buds and 3 to 5 flowers. Small flowers need fine wire; slightly larger flowers, medium wire. Tint the wire leaf green (by same method as dipping stamens) before commencing to mould. Cut into lengths and shape a small hook or knot on the end of each wire (this prevents the flower from slipping off the end of the wire). Have a good supply of prepared wires ready before commencing to mould. Always moisten the wire before inserting into a flower.

Basic Hollow Cone
This shape is the basis for many small flowers. Take a piece of modelling fondant the size of a small pea, and mould to a teardrop shape. Hold the teardrop shape between thumb, index and second fingers and use a knitting needle to hollow out the blunt end. (Rest the cone on the index finger, at the same time rolling the knitting needle around the inside of the cone, concentrating on the edge.)

Drying Flowers
Florist's clay is very handy for supporting small wired flowers while they dry. It is firm and pliable, and wires may be inserted easily. The clay lasts a long time and is not expensive.

To make a Small Spray
Select 2 or 3 buds and 3 to 5 flowers of graduating size. Arrange them with one bud at the top, then two a little further down, then the flowers (from smallest to largest). Hold the wires below the bottom flower and twist wires together firmly, keeping them as straight as possible. Trim ends neatly. Sprays can also be wound with pale green sewing cotton, as described for Lily of the Valley (page 44).

HYACINTHS

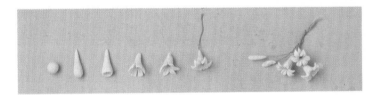

Hyacinth

Hyacinths bloom in all shades of blue, purple, pink, yellow cream and white. They make attractive additions to Christening, bridal and special occasion cakes.

Step 1: Shape a basic hollow cone from a piece of modelling fondant the size of a small pea; cut the cone into six equal petals.

Step 2: Open the petals out lightly with the fingers and use fine scissors to mitre the tips.

Step 3: Insert the knitting needle into the cone and press each petal in turn back gently against the forefinger. This forms a groove down each petal.

Step 4: Insert the prepared moistened wire down into centre of flower and firm flower gently onto the wire. Add short yellow stamens if desired.

To make a bud, mould a small piece of fondant to an oval shape, insert prepared wire and firm base onto wire.

Group one bud and several flowers of graded sizes for a spray.

FORGET·ME·NOT

Forget-me-not

The Forget-me-not is another tiny flower used extensively in decorating. They bloom in various shades of blue; the tiny buds are pale pink, opening to blue. However, for decorating purposes they may be tinted to suit an individual colour scheme.

Step 1: Model a basic hollow cone, then make five equal shallow cuts around the edge.

Step 2: Press the petals flat and smooth any rough edges with fingertips.

Step 3: Insert the moistened, prepared wire into the centre of the flower and firm gently.

Step 4: For the centre, pipe a tiny dot of pale yellow royal icing, or insert a short yellow stamen.

ERIOSTEMON

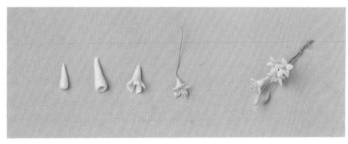

Eriostemon

Eriostemon, a five-petalled Australian pink wax flower, is a delicate addition to floral arrangements. Prepare buds on fine wire and allow to dry.

Step 1: Model a basic hollow cone, then cut the edge into five equal parts.

Step 2: Open the petals out lightly and mitre the tips.

Step 3: Curl the petals back gently and insert the fine prepared wire into the centre of the flower. A spot of water on the wire helps it adhere. Insert several fine stamens (or cottons from the stamens) in the centre of the flower. Form into clusters of several buds and three to five flowers. Use this shape in various sizes as a calyx for other flowers.

BOUVARDIA

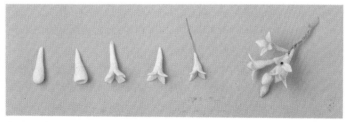

Bouvardia

Bouvardia, a small four-petalled flower with a long trumpet and a green calyx, grows in a cluster or head, in various shades of pink from rosy scarlet to dusty pink, also in yellow, orange-scarlet and white.

Step 1: Shape a long hollow cone and cut the rim into four equal parts (the petals form a cross).

Step 2: Open the flower gently, and round off petal edges with fine scissors.

Step 3: Press the petals gently with thumb and forefinger, smoothing any rough edges. Insert moistened prepared wire, taking care not to harm the long trumpet.

Buds are made as tiny balls with a long trumpet. The base of the trumpet may be painted leaf green to resemble a very tiny calyx if desired.

PENTAS

Pentas

Pentas is a five-petalled flower of the same family as *Bouvardia*; it is made similarly, with five small petals and a white centre. The natural colours are mauve, lilac, red or white. The flower has a long tube and the throat is white or lilac shaded to white.

SNOWFLAKE

Snowflake

Snowflake, more commonly known as Snowdrop, is a six-petalled white flower with a tiny spot of green on each petal.

Step 1: Shape a basic hollow cone and make six equal shallow cuts in the rim.

Step 2: Take the plastic spike and roll the straight end against each petal from the centre to the tip, to form pointed petals. This method takes practice, but once mastered, is more effective than cutting and shaping each petal separately.

Step 3: Place the ball-end of the spike into the centre of the flower and gently fold the petals over the ball to form a bell shape.

Step 4: Insert fine wire, prepared and moistened; firm onto flower.

Two-tier wedding cake: pink Cymbidiums, Stephanotis and pale pink
forget-me-nots decorate this striking cake. Embroidery features tiny
roses, extension work, lace and bluebirds of happiness.

Step 5: When the flower is thoroughly dry, paint a tiny spot of leaf green colouring on each petal towards the tip. Cluster or spray as desired.

LILY OF THE VALLEY

Lily of the valley

This small, dainty flower, is moulded in the same way as the Snowflake, with the addition of a green-tipped stamen for the centre, and the flower is all white. They are used in sprays on various types of cakes. For each spray, prepare a main stem of heavier wire with a bud on hooked (or knotted) end, and two buds moulded onto stamens.

Steps 1-3: As for Snowflake.

Step 4: Insert a moistened green-tipped stamen and allow to dry.

To assemble spray: Take the budded main stem, place the two prepared buds a little way down from the first bud, and wind pale green sewing cotton firmly down the main stem, adding about five flowers (small to larger) alternately. When the last flower has been positioned, wind cotton a little further and secure with a spot of craft glue. Allow to dry.

GYPSOPHILA

Gypsophila

Gypsophila (or Baby's Breath) is a very small starry flower that lends airiness to arrangements. It is essential to use the finest wire, coloured green.

Step 1: Shape a basic hollow cone from a piece of modelling fondant the size of a very small pea and cut the rim into five equal small petals.

Step 2: Using the ball end of the spike, round and shape petals; cup lightly.

Step 3: Place each flower on prepared wire, the end of which has been dampened with water. Very small stamens may be used in the centre, or a spot of yellow royal icing.

Buds are moulded onto longer wires than the flowers. Make a spray of 4 to 5 buds and 3 to 5 flowers.

STEPHANOTIS

Stephanotis

A five-petalled wax flower with a long trumpet, Stephanotis has a ball-shaped bud. It is a very popular flower to mould.

Step 1: Mould a long basic cone from a piece of modelling fondant the size of a small pea and cut rim into five equal petals.

Step 2: Open the petals out slightly and shape each to a rounded point.

Step 3: Turn the petals back gently, insert the fine prepared wire into the centre of the flower, moulding the tube to a long trumpet. Allow to dry.

Step 4: Mould the green calyx in the same way as an Eriostemon flower (page 42) and add to the flower while the calyx is still soft.

The bud, a small ball with a long trumpet, is modelled on fine wire with the calyx added.

SHAMROCK

Shamrock

The small shamrock flower is orchid pink and has five longish egg-shaped petals, veined with a deeper shade of pink; it has a small yellow stamen.

Step 1: Shape a small basic hollow cone and cut rim into five equal petals.

Step 2: Open the petals out lightly and round the tips.

Step 3: Insert fine prepared wire into the centre of the flower. Paint the veins a deeper pink when dry. Make clusters of 3 to 5 flowers and several leaves (pattern page 86).

HONEYSUCKLE

This flower has a long tube, one long petal curving back and four shallow petals, also five long stamens and one very long curved stigma. Colours are pink, cream, gold and variegated.

*Twenty-first birthday cake: colourful pansies and hyacinths are
unusual decorations in the figure-shaped tins. Embroidery features
eyelet work and a shell border.*

Twenty-first birthday cake with formal roses, hyacinths, daisies, key, birds and heart-shaped lace.

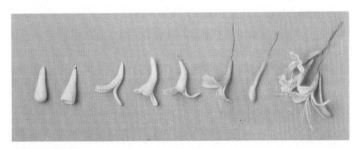

Honeysuckle

Step 1: Cut and hook wire. Mould a long hollow cone and divide the rim into five equal sections. Slash two adjacent cuts fairly deep (for the long petal); the other three cuts are quite shallow.

Step 2: Finger petal tips and round them slightly.

Step 3: Turn the long petal back in a gentle curve; the four small petals also curl back slightly. Insert wire.

Step 4: Curl five stamen cottons and insert in throat of soft flower. Cut one long stamen (for the stigma), shape to a curve over your finger and insert amongst stamens.

AFRICAN VIOLET

African violet

African violets grow in shades of mauve, purple, pink and white; some have colour just around the edges of petals.

The single variety is mainly lilac, but there are many colours in the double blooms.

Step 1: Shape a basic hollow cone and divide rim into one-third and two-third sections.

Step 2: Shape the smaller piece to resemble two joined petals; these petals are about two-thirds the size of the other three (lower) petals.

Step 3: Mould the larger piece to resemble three joined petals. Insert wire.

Step 4: Place four yellow stamens into the centre of the flower.

When dry, wire flowers together to form sprays.

CECIL BRUNNER ROSE

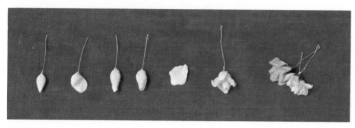

Cecil Brunner rose

This small rose is used extensively on Christening cakes.

Its natural colour is pale pink, but can be tinted as desired. Mould the centres in a slightly darker shade and the outer row of petals paler.

Step 1: Take a small piece of modelling fondant and shape the centre using the flag method (page 28) to form a tight bud. Wire and allow to dry.

Step 2: Mould three small petals, overlap them slightly, and attach each to the bud with a spot of water.

Step 3: The three outer petals are made larger, their side edges curling back. Attach them in the same way.

Step 4: Paint or mould a five-sepal calyx.

ROSE HIP

Rose hips make a realistic addition to an arrangement of roses. They are simple to make and should tone with the colours of the roses.

Step 1: Mould a small ball of modelling fondant, adhere to medium wire and allow to dry.

Step 2: Make a calyx with five sepals in a circle and attach to the *top* of the ball. Twist sepals slightly to look natural.

Step 3: Insert a small group of short cottons in the circle of sepals. Colour to suit the arrangement (see illustration page 30).

7
AUSTRALIAN WILDFLOWERS AND DESIGNS

Australian wildflowers are colourful and lend themselves especially to such occasions as bon voyage parties. Their strong and vibrant colours are shown to best advantage on a neutral-coloured background. Our selection covers the most popular and also some interesting new varieties. They can be combined in many ways, for example: waratah, flannel flowers, wattle and boronia; or Christmas bells, wattle, boronia and Christmas bush.

Designs in the style of Aboriginal rock carvings, or incorporating hand-painted moulded boomerangs, shields, spears and clubs (patterns page 90) also provide interesting decorations. A deep cream-coloured cake, trimmed with fawn or brown ribbon and matching piping, and decorated with a selection of wildflowers, makes a striking centre-piece for any occasion.

MULGA WOOD SHIELDS

Mulga wood boomerang, shield, spears, club; rolled and coloured fondant for mulga wood

Step 1: Roll out a piece of fawn-coloured modelling fondant that has been heavily spotted with brown food colouring; soon there will emerge some very interesting patterns resembling mulga wood.

Step 2: Place the desired pattern (see page 90 for shield, boomerang, etc) over the most interesting part and cut with a sharp scalpel or penknife. Dry over a curved shape. When completely dry, paint with clear water to give a dull satin finish.

FLANNEL FLOWERS

The soft off-white petals of the flannel flower make a con-trast to the vivid colours of many wildflowers. They have about 10 petals and a grey-green centre.

Flannel flowers

Step 1: First mould the dome-shaped centre, 6 mm (about ¼ in) across. Insert prepared medium weight wire and allow to dry for at least 24 hours.

Step 2: When the centre is dry, brush with egg white and dip into caster sugar. Allow to dry again.

Step 3: Take a ball of modelling fondant and mould to teardrop shape.

Step 4: Hollow the wide end with the tapered handle of a paintbrush, skewer, or knitting needle.

Step 5: Cut the rim into halves, then cut each half into five equal parts.

Step 6: Working quickly, mitre each point to about half-way down the petal, to a long slender shape.

Step 7: With brush or knitting needle, press each petal back gently against the forefinger, at the same time slightly grooving the petal. Give some petals a slight twist or an upward lift. Press each tip to a gentle point.

Step 8: Paint a spot of water at the base of the petals and pull the wired centre lightly through; firm it on. Cut off any surplus at back of flower, keeping this part as flat as possible. When dry, tip the end of each petal with a spot of pale green and retouch the centre with the same colour if necessary. Some varieties have green-tipped petals, others have the colour a little way down from the tip.

BORONIA

Brown Boronia is a small flower that can be used as a contrast or to blend in with larger flowers. The size and colour make them attractive additions to most native flower sprays.

A simple birthday cake for a man or boy decorated with flannel flowers, brown boronia, gumnuts and wattle.

Brown boronia

Step 1: Cut and hook wires. Add a tiny ball of modelling fondant to the hook end of each wire and allow to dry.

Step 2: Take a small ball of yellow modelling fondant, mould to teardrop shape.

Step 3: Hollow the blunt end.

Step 4: Cut four rounded petals.

Step 5: Cup the petals around the ball-end of the plastic spike.

Step 6: Moisten the prepared centre, insert into the flower, and firm gently. Cut off any excess.

Step 7: When thoroughly dry, paint the outside of the petals any shade of diluted brown; paint the tiny centre brown.

Buds are formed by moulding tiny balls to a soft point. Cluster flowers loosely and include several wired buds in a spray.

Pink boronia

Pink Boronia, found mainly in New South Wales, is made by the same method as the brown variety, but the petals are softly pointed, not rounded, and the centre has a few tiny stamens.

Step 1: Use pale pink modelling fondant, proceed as for Brown Boronia, cutting petals to a soft point, and cupping as before.

Step 2: Moisten centre with a spot of water, insert the prepared wire and firm flower onto wire; remove surplus from the base of flower.

Step 3: Add 5 to 6 stamen cottons (tinted pale yellow) to the centre of the flower.

Step 4: When thoroughly dry paint the back of the petals a soft (diluted) burgundy.

Buds are tiny plump balls with a point. Mould several onto wires and spray loosely—about five flowers in a cluster.

CHRISTMAS BUSH

Christmas bush is a star-shaped (five petal) flower that blooms in shades of pink, creamy pink and red, and is

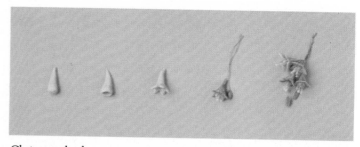

Christmas bush

very popular in most wildflower arrangements.

Step 1: Make a very small basic cone, hollowed out in the usual way.

Step 2: Cut five star-shaped petals.

Step 3: Moisten with a spot of water and insert fine prepared wire.

Step 4: Press each petal out gently in a soft curve.

Step 5: Several tiny stamen cottons may be used in the centre, or a piped dot of yellow royal icing.

Mould several buds on wire and group 3 to 5 flowers in a cluster. The leaves are grouped in threes and finely serrated (pattern page 86).

CHRISTMAS BELLS

Christmas bells

Christmas bells add colour and gaiety to Christmas cakes and they are simple to mould.

Step 1: Take a piece of egg-yellow coloured modelling fondant about the size of an almond and mould to a cone shape.

Step 2: Insert rounded end of skewer and press the cone to a tubular shape, slightly thicker at the base.

Step 3: Cut six short petals and bring each to a soft point. Curve petals back slightly to give a more realistic look. (The depth of the petal is about one-eighth of the length of the tube.)

Step 4: Moisten with a little water, insert a piece of prepared medium wire and firm tube onto the wire.

Step 5: Insert seven yellow stamens (one longer than the others). Allow to dry.

Step 6: Leave the petal tips yellow; paint remainder of tube orange, blending it into the yellow towards the tips. While it is still wet, colour the base of the tube scarlet, blending

Debutantes' cake: fifteen tiny dolls (one for each debutante) each with its own small posy of hyacinths, daisies, Cecil Brunner roses and forget-me-nots; cornelli work adds the finishing touch.

it into the orange. Bend the wires so that the bells hang naturally.

The bud is an elongated teardrop shape, marked with six shallow cuts at the top to resemble the unopened petals. Paint it scarlet, tipped with a little green. Buds vary in size—the new buds are small and point upwards, while the maturing buds are angled outwards.

WATTLE (MIMOSA)

Wattle (mimosa)   Wild cotton

A simple and attractive form of decoration, balls of golden wattle may be moulded and threaded onto wire, piped on wire, or glued on wire. These directions are for the moulded variety.

Step 1: Mould tiny balls of fondant and allow to dry.

Step 2: Place a few drops of yellow colouring in one saucer and some caster sugar in a second saucer.

Step 3: Drop the dried balls into yellow colouring, tumble with a paintbrush; flick into the caster sugar using the paintbrush handle, and then onto waxed paper to dry.

Step 4: Cut a piece of medium covered wire, dip two-thirds into craft glue and press the dried balls onto the wire, covering the wire well.
These flowers are not edible, because of the glue.

WILD COTTON

A bright yellow flower with five heart-shaped petals, and a small darker yellow centre that is surrounded by a mass of fine yellow stamens.

Step 1: Cut five petals and mould to heart shape. Finger the stops and use veining implement to stretch and flute edges slightly.

Step 2: To assemble, pipe a star, arrange petals in spiral fashion.

Step 3: Fill in the centre with yellow stamens.

GUMNUTS

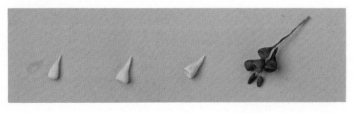

Gumnuts

Step 1: Take a tiny ball of modelling fondant and mould to a teardrop shape.

Step 2: Use a paintbrush handle to hollow out the wide end to a cup shape. Allow to dry and paint any shade of brown. They may be wired if desired with fine wire.

WARATAH

Waratah   Method 1   Method 2

Waratah is a most spectacular flower, mostly coral red, but there is also a rare albino variety in creamy-white.

Method 1

Step 1: Take a ball of dark pink modelling fondant the size of a small walnut, taper slightly to the top; this is known as the *dome*. Embed a piece of heavy hooked or knotted millinery wire into the dome. (The wire must be strong enough to support the weight of the finished flower.)

Step 2: Before the dome sets hard, pierce it all over with a hatpin, making holes right into the centre. (The holes prevent the dome from cracking when it has dried, or even weeks later.) Allow to dry.

Step 3: Using royal icing and No 3 or 4 writing tube, pipe rounded dots; commence with one at the top, surround it with a ring of five, and then pipe larger alternate dots into the spaces for the next row.

Step 4: Pipe the next row of large dots alternately, pulled out and down (like a comma). Continue this way, increasing the pressure to make dots larger until the dome is covered as far as possible. Allow to dry thoroughly.

Step 5: Using undiluted red, scarlet or burgundy (or a mixture of these colours) paint the dome and allow to dry.

Step 6: Using cutters, or a pattern or moulding freehand, make three rows of seven longish petals (really bracts); the first row of smaller petals hug the dome; the next row stand away slightly and the third row of larger petals fall back, curling and twisting to give a natural appearance. Attach each petal with a little water as it is made. When thoroughly dry, paint them the same colour red as the dome. Spot the top of the dome with leaf green. Leaves of the Waratah are very dark green, stiff, shiny and serrated.

Method 2

In this method the Waratah is all moulded. The blossoms of the head are made in advance and allowed to dry.

Step 1: Using pink modelling fondant, mould about 30 small balls and allow to dry.

Step 2: The next shapes are soft commas of three graded sizes. Mould an adequate number of each size—enough to cover the head. Allow to dry.

*Cattleya orchids, hyacinths, maidenhair fern and a painted card
with lace trim decorate this birthday cake—a prize-winner.*

Step 3: Mould the head or dome as in Method 1. While it is still soft, carefully place one small ball on the centre top, a ring of five around it, and another two rows in alternate spaces; adhere each with a spot of water. For the next row commence to use the smallest commas (blossoms); the flat end is inserted into the soft dome, the rounded end points upwards to the top of the dome. Add the next rows in alternate spaces, grading from small to large blossoms, until the dome is almost covered. Allow to dry.

Step 4: Petals or bracts are modelled as in Method 1. Paint flower the required colour.

This method takes longer, but if required for a very special occasion, it is well worth the extra effort.

GENTIAN

Gentian

Gentian is a delicate flower found at high altitudes. It has five soft pointed oval petals which are white, lightly veined with mauve, a five-lobed calyx and five bright golden stamens.

Step 1: Using a small cutter, stamp out five petals.

Step 2: Finger to a soft rounded point.

Step 3: Cup lightly with cushion of a finger, but do not flute.

Step 4: Set to dry in a small foil cup, 25 mm (1 in) diameter.

Step 5: Using a very fine paintbrush, paint veins on the petals in a delicate shade of mauve.

Step 6: Assemble as for single rose and set five heavy gold stamens into the centre. Tip each stamen with a spot of light brown.

The buds are rounded and may be shaded from white to pale mauve. For height, wire some buds and paint a small calyx on them.

COPPER CUPS

Copper Cups (*Pileanthus peduncularis*) are small five-petalled flowers which grow in Western Australia. The flowers range from deep orange for buds to paler shades for older flowers. They have dark centres and stamens (tipped yellow for pollen).

Step 1: Mould a small hollow cone in orange modelling fondant.

Step 2: Cut five equal petals and trim the edges to give a rounded effect.

Step 3: Use the ball-end of the plastic spike to cup and

Copper cups

stretch each petal lightly. Slightly indent the centre with the straight end.

Step 4: Insert moistened prepared wire into the centre of the flower and firm. Add russet stamens while the icing is soft.

Step 5: Paint a spot of green colouring at the base of each petal and touch stamen tips with yellow. Touch up petals.

Copper cups are especially suitable for cakes for men and boys—combined with miniature flannel flowers, brown boronia, burnt orange coloured ribbon and maidenhair fern.

BASIC FOUNDATION FOR PEA FLOWERS

This foundation is used for all wildflowers of the Legume family, such as Broom, Eggs and Bacon, Handsome Wedge Pea, Sturt's Desert Pea, also for the Sweet Pea. Mould a small crescent-shaped bud and insert a hooked or knotted wire. Make required number in advance and allow to dry.

STURT'S DESERT PEA

Sturt's desert pea

Step 1: Using the small frangipani petal cutter, stamp out one base petal, finger edges, fold in halves, moisten and press around the dry pea foundation, the pointed end facing downwards in a soft curve. Remove any surplus paste from the top end to give a smooth rounded effect.

Step 2: Stamp out a second small petal, cut in halves lengthwise, finger each half to crescent shape. Moisten and attach these wing petals, one on either side at rounded end, with tips upturned. Allow this to dry for at least 24 hours.

Step 3: Mould a small ball and place above the wing petals; make an indentation down the centre with the back of a knife. Allow to dry. This section, incorporating the black "boss", is the foundation for the top vertical petal.

Step 4: Cut another small frangipani petal, finger edges, fold in halves lengthwise and crease. Moisten and place the wide end over the "boss" foundation, the tip pointing upwards so it forms a crescent with the base petal; firm gently. Allow to dry.

Twenty-first birthday cake displays Australian wildflowers including Sturt's desert peas, wattle, flannel flowers and a boomerang. Aboriginal motifs have been piped around the sides, with a simple shell scallop at the base.

Step 5: Paint the "boss" black or black with a touch of purple and the petals red.

BROOM
Prepare a small basic pea foundation.

Eggs and bacon; broom; handsome wedge pea

Step 1: Mould pale yellow fondant to make two small wing petals, teardrop shape. Adhere each with a spot of water to the pea base.

Step 2: Mould a larger rounded posterior petal, pinching a fold down the centre. Adhere with a spot of water to the base, firm on and allow to dry.

Step 3: Paint posterior petal yellow; allow to dry. Paint wing petals rust colour. Allow to dry. Use a very fine brush to paint hair lines in rust on the posterior petal, radiating from the base.

Buds may be moulded by adding a closed posterior petal to the base; this is painted a light rust red. Leaves are needle-like clusters.

EGGS AND BACON

Eggs and Bacon is very similar to Broome, except the wing petals are brown and the posterior petal is a paler yellow.

HANDSOME WEDGE PEA

Prepare a pink pea base. Add a small flat wing petal on either side. Wrap a larger heart-shaped posterior petal at the base of the other petals at 90° angle to them.

When dry, paint the base a deeper pink, the inner part of the posterior petal yellow with burgundy radiating out from it. The remainder of the posterior petal and the two small flat wing petals are painted a deep Wedgwood blue. This flower is an appealing contrast to the yellows and reds of most other native flowers.

RUNNING POSTMAN

Running Postman is a larger pea-shaped flower that blooms in bright coral red. Prepare a larger size pea-shaped foundation (pink).

Step 1: Cut a small frangipani petal, finger and fold over the base in a long oval shape which curls out and stands up. Adhere to the base with a spot of water.

Step 2: For the posterior petal, cut a similar shape, finger, fold in halves, crease gently, and adhere to the wire at end of base petal with a spot of water. Curl the petal back gently.

Step 3: When dry, paint the base of the posterior petal a pale leaf green (about one quarter of the petal), then paint the remainder of the flower a bright coral red.

Cocky's tongue; running postman.

COCKY'S TONGUE

Cocky's Tongue is similar to Running Postman but the centre (wing) petal is longer and curves in the opposite direction. It is all red in colour.

NATIVE WILD FLAX

Native wild flax

A small white or pale blue flower of five petals, with hairline threads of deep blue veining the petals and creamy-yellow stamens. Wild Flax is delicate, unusual in colouring and blends well with the more brightly coloured wildflowers.

Step 1: For the centre, make a small white pointed dome shape and insert five short blue stamens and one longer centre stamen. Paint five yellow stripes down the sides of the dome. Allow to dry.

Step 2: Cut five petals using very pale blue modelling paste; finger edges and gently flute, curling the petals slightly. Allow to dry.

Step 3: When dry, paint fine blue lines on each petal with No 00 brush, keeping the centre free of colour.

Step 4: To assemble, pipe a small star of same colour onto foil or waxed paper. Place petals in spiral fashion, add prepared centre piece and allow to dry.

TEA TREE

Tea tree

Tea tree blooms in white, pale pinks and reds. Some have pale green centres. The flowers vary in size from very small to about 25 mm (1 in) diameter.

Step 1: Mould a very small piece of modelling fondant to a hollow cone.

Step 2: Cut five even petals.

Step 3: Using the ball end of the plastic spike, stretch out and cup each petal. Hollow out the centre of the blossom with the blunt end of the plastic spike. Insert wire.

Step 4: When dry, paint the hollow centre a delicate green and pipe a series of very small golden yellow pulled dots in the centre around the base of the petals for stamens. Petals may be painted as desired.

CASSIA

Cassia

Cassia are vivid yellow flowers of the pea family, with cup-shaped petals. They grow mostly in the tropics.

Step 1: Prepare five stamens by dipping the tips of cottons into brown colouring, then into gelatine and leaving to dry. Mould two fine yellow sickle-shapes, allow to dry; paint half the length with brown colouring.

Birthday cake for a boy, features two ponies flooded on a plaque.
Wildflowers finish the decoration—flannel flowers, wattle and
boronia; embroidery is a scattered leaf decoration.

Step 2: Mould three small egg-shaped petals, press against the palm with cushion of the finger to cup them—very little fluting.

Step 3: Mould two slightly narrower petals the same length, curve in the same way and allow to dry. Paint all petals a bright yellow.

Step 4: To assemble, pipe a small star of firm royal icing; set the first three petals close to each other in a half circle at the top, then the two slender petals, slightly apart, at the base.

Step 5: Place the yellow and brown sickle-shapes curving downwards towards the two narrow petals, brown end out. Add a piece of green coloured fine wire about the same length as the sickles, behind them in the centre.

Step 6: Last, place the five chunky stamens in the centre.

HONEY FLOWER
The Honey Flower is long and tubular, with seven tiny

Honey flower

curled-back petals; it blooms in red, pink, cream and yellow.

Step 1: Mould a long tube in white modelling fondant and hollow the centre using a very fine knitting needle.

Step 2: Cut seven small petals and curl them back tightly. Insert wire at the base of the tube.

Step 3: Place a long stamen in the centre. Allow to dry.

Step 4: Colour the outside of the flowers and stamen tips as desired. Arrange in clusters of 5 to 7. Leaves are small and rounded.

8
EXTENSION WORK, LACE AND EMBROIDERY

EXTENSION WORK

Extension work, lace and embroidery

Curtain borders, also called extension or bridgework, are a very distinctive type of decoration used at the base of a cake. The bottom edge is usually scalloped; the top may be varied in shape and design, from a straight tailored edge, to scallops matching the base, heart shapes, points, half moons, etc. It is best to commence piping threads with a No 0 tube and when proficient graduate to 00 and 000 tubes.

Step 1: Pipe a small snail's trail around the base of the cake.

Step 2: Measure the circumference and height of the sides and cut a strip of greaseproof paper this exact size as a pattern.

Step 3: Fold the pattern in halves crosswise, then in quarters and so on until the desired size of a scallop is obtained. Cut a shallow curve through all thicknesses of the pattern to make the scallops. Shape the top of the pattern similarly, as desired. Place the pattern, scalloped side down, around the cake and secure ends of paper with adhesive tape,

keeping the curves of the scallops close to the base. Mark the point of each scallop with a pinprick on the covering fondant. Then carefully mark the top edge of the design in the same way.

Step 4: Using No 2 or 3 writing tube, pipe a row of shallow dropped string scallops between pinpricks. It is important to ensure that the royal icing adheres to the fondant, and then that every subsequent layer adheres to the previous one; breakage can be disheartening when all the strings have been piped. Build out about four or five rows from the cake, allowing each row to dry at least 30 minutes before piping the next. Allow this to dry for several days before commencing Step 5.

Step 5: Use a fine tube (0, 00 or 000) and soft peak icing. Work at eye level. Place the tube on the upper mark and, squeezing evenly, bring the thread out and down, and tuck it under the built out work. The lines are so close together that another line of icing cannot be piped in between any two lines. Neaten the bottom scallops with a tiny rope design, or dots, scallops, etc. Lace pieces may be added later to finish the top edge.

LACE PIECES

Lace pieces may be used with extension work or as a decoration on their own to accentuate features. Suitable designs can be found on embroidery transfers, wallpapers, handkerchief lace, wrought iron, etc. Our basic designs will give you some ideas, but it is rewarding to create your own original designs.

Uniform piping is desirable. Paste a half sheet of graph paper onto a piece of heavy cardboard about 15 x 10 cm (6 x 4 in). Cover this with waxed paper, secured with adhesive tape. Always pipe more lace than required to allow for breakage. To lift the lace use a small rounded knife. Carefully slide the knife under each piece, loosening it from the waxed paper. Lace may be stored for future use, taking care when removing it from waxed paper. Allow for about 100 pieces of lace for a cake 20 cm (8 in) square.

EMBROIDERY

Embroidery is often used on the sides of cakes; it can also be used on the top of a cake if the design so warrants. It is piped freehand using a soft-peak icing; flowers, leaves,

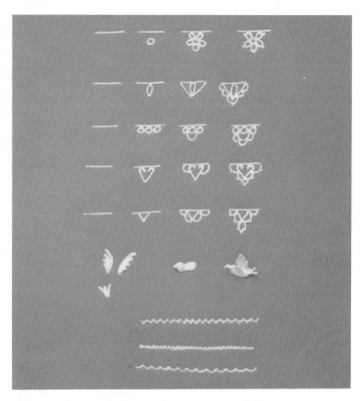

Lace pieces; bluebirds; picot, rope and scalloped edges for extension work

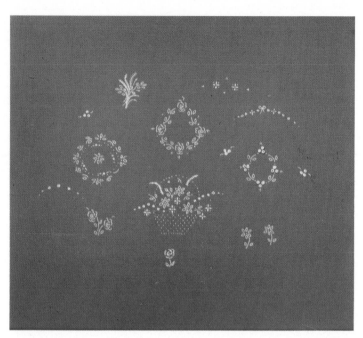

Embroidery

dots, scrolls, etc, can be incorporated. One of the most popular designs is the embossed rose which can be used singly or with other motifs. Designs may be varied by the use of different tubes; for instance Hollyhocks with tiny leaves give emphasis and variety to numerous designs. The designs illustrated are a guide to the countless numbers that a keen decorator may create.

9
PIPED FLOWERS AND FERNS

Piped flowers can be very colourful and attractive; because they are edible they are specially popular for children's cakes. If necessary flowers may be piped several weeks in advance and stored in airtight containers.

Many varieties of flowers can be piped on icing nails greased with white shortening. These give shape and support until the icing is dry. Some decorators prefer to pipe directly onto small squares of waxed paper. Roses are piped on toothpicks, then the toothpick is pierced through a slice of bread covered with waxed paper, leaving the rose to dry on the paper. Storybook (make believe) flowers can be piped in various colours and sizes to suit a particular theme or colour scheme.

Use firm-peak royal icing for all piped flowers. Most flowers are piped with a No 20 petal tube, small, medium or large depending on the size of the flower required. When thoroughly dry, remove flower from the icing nail by applying very gentle heat (such as a match) for several seconds to melt shortening; then lift the flower off and store in a covered container.

To wire piped flowers, allow to dry, then turn flower face down and pipe a bulb on the back. Insert hooked wire and support until dry.

Piped flowers

Icing nails used for piped flowers

TO PIPE A BASIC PETAL

Use a No 20 petal tube, hold the bag at a 45° angle with the wide end of the tube to the centre, and revolve the greased nail anti-clockwise, while squeezing gently to form a shallow cupped petal. By varying the pressure, the angle of the tube and icing colour, many varieties of flowers may be made with the one tube, using this basic method (see page 20).

PIPED ROSE

Cover a thin slice of bread with waxed paper and secure with adhesive tape.

Step 1: Hold a wooden toothpick in the left hand with

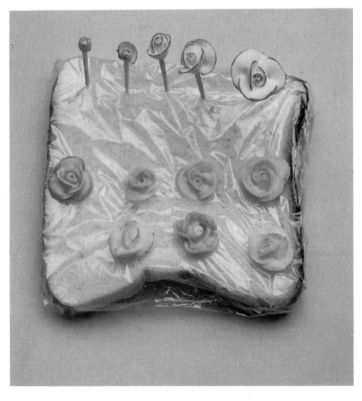

Piped rose

the broad end pointing upwards and the long point of the No 20 tube touching the flat side of the toothpick. Squeeze the bag whilst revolving the toothpick anti-clockwise.

Make one complete turn of the toothpick to form the tight bud, which is the heart of the rose.

Step 2: Tilt the toothpick downwards. Pipe two petals commencing from the base of the bud (one on either side), moving the point of the tube up and then down in a horse-shoe movement. At this stage it may be used as a bud if required. Add three or four petals for the full rose, using the same movement. Commence to pipe each petal one-third of the way behind the previous petal. Add an extra petal for balance if necessary.

Step 3: Remove from the toothpick by inserting the pointed end through the prepared bread and allow the rose to sit on the waxed paper until dry.

ROSEBUD

Rosebuds may be piped directly onto a cake, or onto waxed paper and transferred when dry.

Step 1: Using a large writing tube, pipe a teardrop shape.

Step 2: Turn teardrop upside-down and overpipe the teardrop with a figure 'S'.

Step 3: Pipe a green calyx.

BLOSSOM

Blossom

Icing nails are generally used for blossom.

Step 1: Grease the flat top of the nail with a little white shortening. Pipe a small dot to centre the flower.

Step 2: Using No 20 petal tube, hold the bag at a 45° angle with the long end of the tube to the centre; revolve the nail anti-clockwise, squeezing gently to form a rounded, slightly cupped petal.

Step 3: Pipe four more petals, each overlapping, to form a circle.

Step 4: Pipe tiny dots in the centre or one larger dot surrounded by a circle of small dots. Small stamens, cottons dipped in gelatine or pearl stamens may also be used for the centre.

DAISY

Daisy

Daisies may be piped in any size and a variety of colours, as Cinerarias, Livingstone Daisies, small or large Marguerites, and so on.

Step 1: Pipe a centre dot on the nail. Commencing from the outer edge of the nail, pipe a long rounded petal with a downward stroking movement towards the centre.

Step 2: The next petal is commenced close beside (almost under) the previous one. There is no set number of petals for a daisy, but it is better not to overcrowd.

Step 3: For the centre, pipe a series of tiny yellow dots with an extra dot at the base of each petal.

DOUBLE DAISY

These are made in the same way as a single daisy, with an additional row of petals. Pipe the first row of petals and allow to dry before piping the second row on top, petals alternating. Fill in the centre with small dots as before.

DAHLIA

Dahlias are piped in all shades, including variegated colours. They are easy to pipe and look impressive amongst a spray of piped flowers. Before attaching a tube to the screw, pipe a small dome of icing and allow to dry. This gives shape to the flower, allowing the petals to be raised.

Step 1: Attach the petal tube and commence piping, using the same narrow petal shape as for the daisy (petals commence from the outer edge of the nail, easing to the centre). Complete a circle of petals which are flat on the nail, within the outer edge.

Step 2: Pipe the next round of petals on top, holding the tube at a 45° angle.

Step 3: Pipe another circle of petals, holding the tube at a 90° angle.

Step 4: Pipe the centre row of petals to stand up.

Step 5: A series of pulled dots forms the centre, or stamens may be used.

CARNATION

Carnation

Carnations are piped using stiff royal icing to create a broken petal edge. Their colours range from white and pastels to vibrant shades; they can also be variegated. First pipe a small dome in the centre of the nail, without a tube on the bag.

Step 1: Attach No 20 tube. Squeeze the icing bag and, while piping, use a jiggling movement to give a wavy effect. Pipe five or six large petals flat on the nail to make a circle.

Step 2: Holding the tube at a 45° angle, pipe the second row of petals in alternate spaces.

Step 3: Pipe a third row of petals as Step 2.

Diamond-shaped two-tier wedding cake featuring blue daisies,
forget-me-nots and a bird bath.

Step 4: Pipe the centre three petals in an almost upright position.

The completed flower should be rounded, consisting of three rows of five or six petals, plus three centre petals.

CORNFLOWER

Step 1: Pipe a small dome of icing in the centre of the nail. Attach No 5 star tube. With icing coloured dark blue, pipe a series of pulled stars to cover the dome.

Step 2: Change to No 1 writing tube and paler blue icing; pipe a series of pulled dots over centre stars.

Step 3: Add dark blue stamens amongst the star petals to soften the effect.

PINCUSHION

Pincushions are made in the same way as Cornflowers; using No 1 or No 2 writing tube, cover the dome with pulled dots in various shades of blue; add a few stamens in a toning colour or white.

SCOTCH THISTLE

Step 1: Using green icing, pipe a small dome on waxed paper.

Step 2: Attach No 1 writing tube (with mauve icing) and overpipe a series of radiating lines.

Step 3: With green icing, pipe pulled dots over the green dome to resemble thorns or prickles. When thoroughly dry, retouch with a darker shade of green, using a paint-brush.

The thistle leaf is piped on waxed paper; it has spiky points piped as pulled dots. Allow to dry, then flood, using the paintbrush method. Retouch with darker green to match the flower.

WISTERIA

Wisteria

Wisteria may be piped directly onto the cake or onto waxed paper, lifted when dry and placed in clusters, with piped tendrils and leaves, on the cake. Use firm-peak icing, mauve coloured, and a No 20 small tube.

Step 1: Place the long end of the tube downwards, holding the bag at 90° angle. Commence piping at the tip of the flower: squeeze and pull to make a petal about 6 mm (¼ in) long.

Step 2: Make another petal on either side of the first, starting about half-way down.

Step 3: Make another three petals slightly below the second row. This stage may be used as a bud.

Step 4: Pipe four petals across the base, all petals finishing at a centre point. Reduce the next row of petals to three, and the final row to two.

LUPIN

Lupins are made in the same way as Wisteria, in yellows, pinks and blues.

SWEET PEA

Sweet pea

Sweet peas piped on nails are simple and effective. Pipe them in bright colours, pastels or variegated.

Step 1: Pipe the first petal in a horseshoe shape, flat on the nail, whilst turning the nail anti-clockwise and jiggling the tube slightly to give a fluted edge.

Step 2: Pipe the second petal in the same way, holding the tube at a 45° angle which makes the petal stand up.

Step 3: The third petal (or keel) is piped at a 90° angle (holding the bag upright) in the centre of the flower, while pressing and easing to the base. All petals finish at the same point.

Step 4: Change to No 1 writing tube and green icing and pipe a calyx. Green tendrils may be added when the flowers are attached to the cake.

PANSY AND VIOLA

Pansy

Pansies (yellow, gold, brown, blue, purple, burgundy, cream) are colourful additions to pipework and are fairly easy to master. Several colours may be placed in the one bag (e.g., purple and orange, with yellow at the long side of the tube) and when piped attractive colour combinations and patterns emerge. They have five petals, two sets of two and a large single petal.

Step 1: Pipe the right-hand basic petal, flat onto the nail.

Step 2: Pipe the left-hand petal similarly.

Step 3: Repeat Steps 1 and 2 for the two top petals, slightly overlapping the first two.

Step 4: Place the point of the pipe into the centre of the flower, squeeze firmly and revolve the nail anti-clockwise, to form one large base petal.

Step 5: Pipe a large pulled dot for the centre, or add a yellow stamen.

Step 6: When dry, use a very fine brush to paint lines on the bottom petal, radiating from the centre.

Violas are piped in the same way, using a smaller tube and mauve, blue and yellow icing.

VIOLET

Step 1: Use a greased icing nail. Hold the pipe vertically and move it lightly up and down to form two slender upper petals.

Step 2: Pipe three lower petals slightly larger.
Pipe the violet in white icing and when dry paint the petals, leaving the centre white. When the dark colour is dry, paint in a yellow centre or add a yellow stamen. Wood violets are all white or pale pink.

NARCISSUS: JONQUIL AND DAFFODIL

The bright cheerful faces of the Narcissus group, daffodils and jonquils, lend themselves to many decorating themes. Their variations of colour and size give wide scope.

Jonquils are piped with six basic petals of equal size.

Step 1: Mark the centre of the nail with a dot. Use a No

Twin hearts engagement cake featuring spring flowers—jonquils, daffodils, daisies, violets, snowflakes and jasmine. Piped scallops and embroidery complete the decoration.

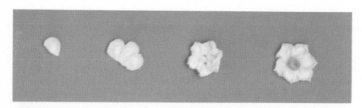

Narcissus

20 petal tube (medium), held at a 45° angle. Pipe six petals, each commencing from the centre of the nail, moving out to the edge and back to the centre.

Step 2: While the icing is wet, gently pinch each petal to a point.

Step 3: Change to No 1 or 2 writing tube for the trumpet. Commence with a small dot and overpipe to form a small cone. Allow to dry. Brush a touch of very pale green colour around the base of the petals.

Daffodils are piped as for Jonquils, but the trumpet is much larger and has a fluted edge. Overpipe the cone with a zigzag movement to give this ruffled look. When dry, tint as desired. The trumpet may be piped yellow, orange or salmon pink. Daffodils combined with tiny daisies and violets make most attractive posies.

CORNCOB

Corncobs add colour to arrangements. They can be used effectively on thanksgiving or harvest festival cakes, or combined with simple piped flowers. Use a very firm yellow icing and No 5 or 8 star tube.

Step 1: For each corncob, pipe a shell on waxed paper.

Step 2: Change to No 1 or 2 writing tube. Turn the shell upside-down and pipe five snail's trails: one down the centre, one down each side, and two more rows in between, to completely cover the shell.

Step 3: Change to fawn-coloured icing and No 00 tube and pipe a silk tassel coming from the top.

Step 4: For the husk, add a little brown to some green icing in the bag to give a two-toned effect. Using No 16 or 17 tube, pipe one long leaf on either side of the cob, commencing at the base and working up to a point.

GRAPES

Step 1: Using very firm royal icing and a No 5 or 8 star tube, pipe a teardrop-shaped shell. Change to No 2 or 3 writing tube.

Step 2: Commencing from the point, pipe a series of pulled dots (not in straight rows) until the dome is completely covered.

Grapes may be piped onto waxed paper, allowed to dry and then placed on the cake, or piped directly onto the surface. The addition of tendrils and leaves gives a finishing touch. Usual colours are green, purple or variegated; a combination of mauve, yellow, green and brown, all in the one bag, brings out many interesting patterns. White grapes may also be piped on wedding cakes for variety of design.

TOOTHPICK FLOWERS

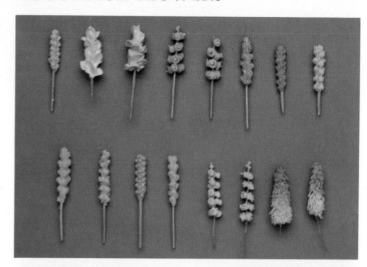

Toothpick flowers

Spiked flowers, piped on toothpicks, lend themselves to children's cakes, particularly ones for little girls. They are quick and easy to pipe and colours can be just as bright as you choose.

Red Hot Pokers: Pad the toothpick with royal icing or modelling fondant to resemble a small upturned carrot; allow to dry. Using yellow royal icing, pipe a series of pulled dots to cover the foundation. When dry, brush on colour, graded from yellow at the base to diluted orange and a red tip.

Green Pokers are piped in the same way; the yellow is retouched with a little lime green at the tip.

Stocks are piped with an up-and-over movement to form tiny petals. Pipe a series of petals about one-third of the way down the toothpick. Use any pastel colours, or variegated, or grade colour from pale to darker down the toothpick.

By using various tubes and colours, lavender, lilac and lupins may also be simulated by this method.

FLOWERS PIPED ON WIRE

Lily of the Valley

These small delicate flowers, piped directly onto wire, add a touch of airiness or lightness to arrangements. Cut a piece of fine wire about 5 cm (2 in) long, curve it gently and lay flat on waxed paper.

Step 1: Using No 2 writing tube and white royal icing, pipe a series of five graded dots down the wire.

Step 2: Around the bottom edge of each dot, pipe three tiny dots to resemble petal tips.

*Two-tier scalloped oval wedding cake (baked in specially-made tins)
has a simple scalloped edge which incorporates the fleur-de-lis.
Moulded bells on the sides blend in with the hollyhock embroidery,
two bands of ribbon. The Phalaenopsis orchid is the feature flower
of this cake.*

Step 3: When dry, turn the wire over and repeat Steps 1 and 2 on the other side, to make bells rounded.

Forget-me-nots

Prepare a strand of fine wire, curve slightly and place on waxed paper.

Step 1: Using No 1 writing tube and pale blue royal icing, pipe five small dots in a circle, touching each other.

Step 2: Pipe a yellow dot for the centre.

Step 3: Allow to dry before lifting, then pipe a small dot of royal icing on the back of the flower to prevent separation from the wire.

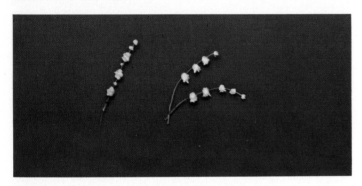

Forget-me-nots; lily of the valley

Hollyhocks

Hollyhocks are graded in size down the wire stem from small to large. They may be piped in any desired colour or combinations of colours.

Step 1: Attach No 1 tube. Cut small lengths of fine wire. Push the wire into the tube, squeeze while removing the wire, which will be covered with royal icing.

Step 2: Place wire on the waxed paper and commence piping from the top, three small graded dots for buds. For the first bell pipe a small cone (a small circle, overpiped several times). Continue bells towards the bottom of the stem, grading to slightly larger. Dry, turn wire over and pipe a row of bells on the other side.

Step 3: When dry, pipe flowers alternately down the sides for a three-dimensional effect.

Step 4: When dry, pipe a contrasting pulled dot in the centre of each bell.

FERNS

Ferns

Maidenhair

Cut three pieces of fine wire, tint brown and curve gently. Lay them side by side on waxed paper.

Step 1: Pipe a series of pale green graded dots down each wire. Allow to stand for a few seconds, then place a small square of waxed paper over each frond. Gently press flat. Leave the paper in position until dry and ready for use.

Step 2: Carefully peel off the paper. Retouch with a damp brush if more colour is necessary. Pierce a hole in the cake with a hatpin and insert the three fronds into it, using long tweezers. Handle with care.

Fishbone Fern

This flat fern, piped on wire, is useful in arranging with flowers.

Step 1: Use green coloured icing and No 1 or 2 writing tube. Insert the wire into the writing tube and squeeze the bag gently, withdrawing the wire; it will be covered with royal icing, making subsequent piping easier.

Step 2: Place the icing-covered wire on waxed paper, and with a diagonal zigzag movement, pipe the fern down one side of the wire; repeat the process on the other side. The tiny leaves match in size on either side.

Bracken

Step 1: Use the same method as for Fishbone to cover the wire.

Step 2: Using No 1 tube and variegated icing, shape the frond as illustrated.

10
FLOODING OR RUN-IN WORK

Flooding or run-in work is a technique for filling in outlined designs with colour. Three-dimensional effects (e.g. for facial features) may be achieved by building layer upon layer, allowing each to dry in between.

A wide variety of designs may be used, but it is wise at first to choose simple, clear outlines. Children's books, postcards, gift-wrappings are excellent sources of inspiration. Simple motifs may be used on all types of cakes, for instance a vintage car is appropriate for a boy's twenty-first birthday cake or a nursery design for a Christening cake.

Designs may be cut out in modelling fondant, gum paste or pastillage and then flooded and placed on the cake; or outlined on a plaque and then flooded; or pinpricked directly onto the cake and flooded. Small designs may be outlined on waxed paper (using an 00 tube) and flooded; when dry, tiny details are painted (with colour) onto the design, and the design placed on the cake. If the motif is to be used on the curved side of a cake, dry it over a curved surface.

PLAQUES

Use modelling fondant, gum paste or pastillage. Roll out a quantity to about 2mm ($^1/_{16}$ in) and cut a shape, using a saucer as a guide (cut several extras to practise on). Roll carefully to ensure a smooth surface and use the dampened point of a craft knife or razor blade when cutting to obtain a neat edge. Allow to dry on a flat surface for several days, turning frequently. When dry, carefully sandpaper the surface and edges to give a smooth finish. Plaques keep indefinitely if stored in a dry place.

Pastillage

Pastillage, a mixture of royal icing and gum tragacanth, is useful for modelling where strength is required, e.g., for houses, churches, etc, as it sets firmly in humid weather. Buy powdered gum tragacanth from a chemist (it may have to be ordered in).

Sprinkle ½ teaspoon of powdered gum tragacanth into 1 cup of well-worked royal icing and beat thoroughly with a knife. Place in an airtight container and allow to stand for 24 hours. Then remove from the container and add enough sifted pure icing sugar to form a pliable dough; knead well. Store in a plastic bag inside an airtight container until ready for use (do not store in a refrigerator).

Flooded plaques

Colour as desired, allowing dark colours to mature for several hours before use.

Gum Paste

500 g (1 lb) pure icing sugar
2 teaspoons gelatine
¼ cup boiling water

Sift icing sugar. Thoroughly dissolve gelatine in boiling water, add to half the quantity of icing sugar in a large bowl. Knead well, adding more of the icing sugar till the mixture is no longer sticky. Keep in a plastic bag in a screw-top jar—it dries quickly. Colour as required.

Note: Use gum paste for simple shapes that can be modelled quickly; it is not recommended for flowers. Dust hands and work surface with maize cornflour before handling it.

Children's handkerchiefs can provide designs for birthday cakes.
Here the background and the bear on a swing were flooded, and
piped jonquils, butterflies and rabbits were dried and then placed
on the cake.

PREPARING DESIGN OUTLINE

Step 1: Trace the selected design onto greaseproof paper, turn the paper over and pencil the design on the reverse side.

Step 2: Turn the paper back to the original side and centre it on the plaque.

Step 3: With a sharp pencil, and taking care not to smudge the outline, trace over the design, then lift the paper. The design will be outlined on the plaque. (Note that pencilled outlines are used on plaques only as pencil lead is not edible.)

Step 4: Use No 1 tube for general work or 0 or 00 for tiny motifs. Fill the bag with royal icing and outline the design; allow to dry.

PREPARING COLOURS

Thin a small quantity of royal icing with strained lemon juice or egg white to a thick cream consistency. (To test consistency, drop a spoonful back into the mass and count to 10; the icing should be smooth again.) If using red, thin icing down just with red colouring direct from the bottle. Colour icing in small quantities—a little goes a long way.

APPLYING COLOUR

Flood each outlined section and allow for drying time, otherwise colours run into each other; take special care when using red alongside white. In general, work background detail first, major foreground detail last. Use a brush to transfer icing into an outlined section in the same way as an artist uses paints. Fill each section to the edge. Take care to avoid air bubbles; brush away any that appear.

Painted plaques

HANDPAINTING

Designs may also be painted directly onto the covering fondant. Choose a simple outline, cut a paper outline pattern and place it on the cake. Using a very fine brush, trace around the shape using diluted colouring; remove the pattern. Carefully paint in details, allowing drying time for each colour. As you work, use a practice piece of covering fondant to test colours and moisture, as too much liquid on the brush could ruin the covering.

11
CHRISTMAS DECORATIONS

Decorations for a Christmas cake may be elaborate or very simple. Designs can include cards, candles, bells, holly, brightly coloured gifts, boots with fluffy tops, angels, trees decorated with garlands, toys, etc. For ideas look at wrapping paper, children's books and Christmas cards.

Christmas decorations

CHRISTMAS CARD

Roll out a piece of modelling fondant about 10 x 23 cm (4 x 9 in), and fold carefully in half, taking care not to press the crease because the fondant will crack. Decorations may be three-dimensional—for instance, poinsettias with candles and holly leaves; Christmas roses, pine cones and holly; Father Christmas; a Nativity scene provides a colourful display for experienced decorators.

BELLS

Roll out a piece of fondant the same shape as the doll's skirt (pattern page 94) and ease gently into the bell mould. Lightly moisten edges. Allow to dry thoroughly before removing. Some wine glasses make good bell moulds if plastic moulds are not available.

SUGAR BELLS

Moisten crystal sugar with a small amount of egg white to the consistency of wet sand, colour and press into a clean plastic bell mould. Turn out gently onto a flat, clean surface and allow the bell to stand for a short time. When you are able to pick up the bell, turn it upside-down and carefully scrape excess sugar from the inside. With practice, bells may be scraped out to a thickness of 3 mm (⅛ in). When dry, paint the edge of the bell with egg white and sprinkle with edible glitter.

EDIBLE GLITTER

Edible glitter, made from gum arabic and water, adds variety and sparkle to Christmas decorations. Chemists usually stock gum arabic or will order it in.

To Make Edible Glitter

Place 2 tablespoons of cold water in a double saucepan and sprinkle 50 g (2 oz) gum arabic on top. Heat gently, stirring until dissolved. Colour as desired. Strain through a piece of muslin or cheesecloth and brush onto a clean scone tray. Place the tray in a cool oven (140°C/275°F) to dry. When dry, scrape the tray with a knife and flake glitter between the fingers. Store in a jar.

BOOTS

Cut out the boot pattern and flood red, brown or black. Allow to dry. Finish the top with medium-peak royal icing, applied with a paintbrush, to resemble ruffled fur.

PARCELS

Mould small square or oblong pieces of paste, paint them bright colours, allow to dry. Tie with narrow tinsel ribbon.

CANDLES

These can be modelled in different lengths and widths, tapered or straight, and the design may incorporate candle holders. They can either stand up on the cake or lie flat, surrounded with flowers and ribbons. Pipe royal icing to resemble wax dripping down the sides, add a yellow flame and streaks of light in a circle around it.

CHRISTMAS TREES

Trees are piped over a cardboard cone which has been

*Christmas cake: Father Christmas has been flooded directly onto
the cake. The herringbone shell edge, and tiny sprigs of holly with
matching red ribbon, complete a simple cake for beginners.*

Christmas cake: wildflowers combined with a spear, club and shield, Aboriginal motifs piped on the sides, and a dancing lady border.

painted with royal icing thinned with egg white. Using firm-peak icing and the leaf pipe, commence piping rows at the base of the cone; work alternate rows in the opposite direction. Pipe leaves larger at the base, grading to smaller at the top. The tree may stand in a gaily coloured tub of modelling fondant, or on a cut-out shape laid flat on the cake. Garlands and baubles, silver cachous, gaily wrapped parcels and edible glitter all give a colourful finish.

HOLLY LEAVES

A quick and easy method for cutting out holly leaves requires a plastic ballpoint pen top or a small petal cutter. Roll out a piece of green modelling fondant and stamp out seven or eight circles around the edge, leaving a spiky leaf shape. Vein the leaf with the back of a penknife. Dry the leaves with a twist or a turn and then paint over with dark leaf-green colouring. Roll the small cut-out circles into balls and when dry paint them bright red, for berries.

12
EASTER EGGS

Easter eggs make attractive gifts and can be decorated effectively with small piped or moulded flowers, ribbon loops, etc. The eggs can be made from chocolate, sugar (as for sugar bells, page 72), gum paste, modelling fondant or marshmallow. Moulds are obtainable prior to Easter at specialty decorating stores or large department stores. It is also possible to buy hollow chocolate eggs suitable for decorating. Choose smooth-finished eggs for preference. Designs may be flooded onto chocolate eggs or painted onto modelling fondant eggs; motifs may be dried over a curve and placed on the egg.

TO TEMPER CHOCOLATE

For the best handling results, temper chocolate as follows. Grate the chocolate and place in a double boiler. Using a confectionery thermometer, heat to 38-46°C (100-115°F), stirring constantly. Remove from heat, stand top pan in cold water, and bring the temperature down to 27-28°C (80-82°F), stirring well. Replace the top pan over hot water and heat to 31-32°C (88-90°F), stirring well. The chocolate is now ready for use. For milk chocolate use 2°F (1°C) lower temperature in each case.

CHOCOLATE EGGS

Step 1: Wipe inside of mould with a clean soft cloth, making sure not to scratch the surface as this will be the outside of the egg and any marks will be visible.

Step 2: Pour the tempered chocolate carefully into the two half-egg moulds, making sure the inside is well covered with chocolate. Pour the surplus back into the pan. Allow to set in a cool place (not in the refrigerator). When firm, remove from the mould with care and join the two halves with melted chocolate.

Decorating Hints

For easier handling, and to avoid breakage of lace decorations and flowers, the egg may be placed on a stand of solid chocolate. Fill a small party mould with melted chocolate and allow to set. When firm, remove it from the mould and attach to the egg with a spot of melted chocolate.

To pipe with melted chocolate, add 2-3 drops glycerine or 1 teaspoon sugar syrup for every 125 g (4 oz) of chocolate. Paper icing bags may be used for this type of work.

Easter eggs

13
ORNAMENTS AND TRIMMINGS

Cakes of today are simple and elegant. Hand-made ornaments look more in keeping with hand-moulded sugar flowers, than plastic and other artificial flowers do. Elegant cakes demand elegant floral arrangements. Many motifs may be used effectively on wedding cakes: small or large bells, embroidered and lace trimmed; bells with flowers spilling out; small baskets, bowls, or vases of flowers; fluted or scalloped shells; ring cases; fountain or bird bath; harp or lyre; Bible and rosary beads; horseshoe, etc.

Try to develop an individual style of arranging so that each of your cakes has its own distinctive quality.

Some brides request a lasting memento incorporated in the design, perhaps a small silver goblet or liqueur glass filled with flowers, or a bridal slipper filled with flowers.

Wedding ornaments

FROSTED GLASS

Liqueur glasses or small clear plastic containers may be painted to give the appearance of frosted glass. Thin the royal icing to a runny consistency with acetic acid and paint it on the glass. Pipe grapes on the flat base or wisteria or cornelli. Arrange small flowers in the glass with ribbon loops and tulle or place them around the base. When arranging flowers in bowls, baskets, shells or slippers, etc, place a small piece of *covering fondant* in the container and secure with royal icing; this provides a firm base for floral work and does not set too hard. Stand for 24 hours before arranging the flowers.

BELLS

Select a good bell mould; some wine or champagne glasses are a suitable substitute; the rim must be the widest part in order to remove bell without damaging it.

Method 2

Wipe the mould with a soft cloth and dust freely with cornflour. Take a piece of modelling fondant large enough to cover the mould; roll out and cut to doll's skirt pattern (see page 94). Join the two straight edges of the bell, moistening with water and ease gently into the shape of the mould. Care must be taken to press the bell gently, as it could stick to the mould. While it is still soft, turn it out to make sure it is free, then return to the mould to set. The seam is camouflaged with flowers, ribbons, etc, held in place with covering fondant. The outside of the bell may be covered with cornelli or embroidery or left plain. Edges are finished with piped lace, a dainty shell border or pearl stamens attached with royal icing.

Large bells may have fancy trims such as slots for threading ribbon or picot edgings; these are cut while the bell is soft. Allow to dry thoroughly before removing from the mould and decorating. If the clapper is to be covered with cornelli or forget-me-nots (or other tiny flowers) first cover the wire with royal icing (by inserting the wire into the icing tube). When dry, attach a small ball of modelling fondant to end of wire, allow to dry, then add the small flowers. The wire can also be bound with narrow satin ribbon. Attach end of wire to inside of bell with a spot of royal icing and support with cotton wool until dry.

Small bells may be cut in halves while soft, dried and placed on the sides of cakes in pairs. Very small whole bells may be tied in groups of three and placed on the cake—remember to cut slots for the thread when moulding the bells.

BASKETS

Small baskets are cut in modelling fondant with a fluted biscuit cutter and set in a patty pan or mould; party shape

Individual doll cakes for children's parties can be easily made and
decorated. Bake the cakes in individual pudding steamer bowls.
Butter cake, marble cake or fruit cake mixture is suitable.

cutters may also be used. Pipe with cornelli or embroidery and finish with flowers and ribbon loops. Handles are made with several pieces of twisted wire firmly bound with ribbon (secured at each end of the handle with a stitch). Insert a small piece of covering fondant in basket and firm ends of handle into the fondant. Allow to dry before arranging flowers. Do not overcrowd the shape with too many flowers.

FOUNTAIN OR BIRD BATH

Using a fluted biscuit cutter, cut a circle of modelling fondant and press into a patty tin. Cut the base to the size of a 20 cent piece and set in a patty tin to curve slightly. Roll a stem to pencil thickness and about 30 mm (1¼ in) long. Cut two small discs about the size of a 1 cent piece. Allow to dry.

To make up: Attach one small disc to centre of curved base with royal icing. Then attach stem, second small disc, and base of bowl similarly. Check that it is straight. Support the fountain with cotton wool or tissues until set. When dry, decorate as desired.

BOWL

A small bowl can be made in similar fashion to fountain, attaching fluted bowl directly to base.

HARP

Paint or spray a length of wire gold. Cut two shapes from the pattern (page 88) and allow to dry. Cut wire into 25 graded pieces. Pipe a line of royal icing along top of one shape and arrange wires carefully in position. Pipe royal icing to attach second shape, sandwiching the wires in between; allow to dry. Roll a pencil-thick piece of fondant about 8 cm long and push a piece of strong wire through the centre, protruding about 1 cm from end; allow to dry.

Attach top and bottom with royal icing. Pipe tiny shells to fill in the join around the frame. Decorate with fine cornelli. Retouch with gold.

LYRE

The lyre is made in a similar fashion to the harp, attaching wires at top with a strip of modelling fondant. Decorate as desired.

BIBLE, ROSARY BEADS AND CROSS

Bible: Cut a thick rectangular slab from firm modelling fondant; prick top and bottom all over with a needle and allow it to dry. Paint three edges with gold or silver. Roll out fondant cover and cut a rectangle to wrap around the first slab, overlapping slightly. Attach to first slab with a spot of water. Allow to dry. Decorate with a cross or as desired.

Rosary Beads are made of tiny balls of modelling fondant, threaded while soft onto fine cotton, using a needle. Colour or tint when dry if desired.

Cross: A small moulded cross may be attached to the Bible or rosary beads. Colour it with gold or silver enamel if desired.

CRYSTALLIZED FLOWERS

Small blossoms—tiny roses, gypsophila, African violets, hyacinths, or single petals of roses—can be preserved in caster sugar crystals; they will last indefinitely.

Beat an egg white lightly, then paint this onto the flower, making sure it is completely covered. Sprinkle liberally with caster sugar to coat all surfaces. Shake to remove excess sugar. Dry at room temperature or for 15 minutes in a very low oven. Store in an airtight container, separated with crumpled waxed paper.

14
MARZIPAN FRUIT AND VEGETABLES

Marzipan fruits make an ideal gift with a personal touch. They may be made using the recipe on page 22, or using leftover undercoating from a cake. Most health food stores sell prepared almond icing or almond paste, which is suitable for moulding into fruits or vegetables.

Take one quantity of marzipan and colour it pale yellow—a good basic colour with which to commence. Most fruit or vegetables require an extra touch of colour to give them a realistic look. It is good to have fruit from which to copy, if they are in season. Mould the fruit in one-bite or two-bite sizes, erring on the smaller size. Allow it to stand for several days to dry and firm before painting.

Marzipan fruits and vegetables

Orange: Commence with a small ball, imprint the rind with a fine grater and paint with orange colouring.

Pear: The pear is also moulded from a small ball, gradually tapering at the top. Break a dried clove in half, pressing the bud into the broad end of the pear, the stick into the narrow end to resemble a stalk. Paint a touch of diluted red on the rounded section to give the appearance of ripeness.

Apple: An apple is modelled from a ball, this time with the sides gently curved. Use a clove in the same way as for a pear. Streak the apple with light red to resemble a Delicious apple, or add more red for a Jonathan and colour green for a Granny Smith.

Banana: Shape a curved roll, thinner towards the ends. Paint a few brown streaks for a ripe effect.

Lemon: Lemons are moulded in a ball, easing out to a soft point at each side. Tint the points green.

Strawberry: These are moulded again from a ball which tapers to a rounded point. Paint red colouring straight from the bottle and drop the strawberry into crystal or caster sugar while wet. Add a small green leaf of moulded marzipan.

Apricot and Peach: Shape into a ball; make an imprint with the back of a small knife, half-way around the fruit. Colour desired shade.

Watermelon (slice): Mould a flat circle, then cut in halves and leave to dry. Tint the curved skin dark green, leave a small natural-coloured strip, then paint the flat sides and straight edge deep pink. Seeds may be added by painting dark brown spots on the pink.

Cherries: Cherries are also moulded as small balls; stamens are used to represent stalks. The stalks are tinted green and tied in small bunches, the cherries painted deep red.

Carrots and Parsnips: Carrots and parsnips are moulded from a ball, tapered to a long point. Mark light ridges with the back of a knife. Paint the carrots orange, leave parsnips the natural shade. Add a sprig of parsley for the leaves.

Peas: Peas are small green balls, placed in a boat-shaped pod.

Mushrooms: Mushrooms are simple to make—two rounds of marzipan, one thinner and slightly larger than the other. The larger piece is placed over the smaller round (which has been tinted pale pink) and the two are cupped to shape. Slash the pink lightly and add a stalk.

Pumpkin: This is a colourful addition to a collection of marzipan. Make a ball, flatten slightly at the top and bottom; mark grooves with the back of a knife. Cut out a wedge and leave to dry; paint the inside orange, the skin dark green.

15
HANDY HINTS

1. Bake the cake 6-8 weeks in advance of decorating to allow it to mature.

2. A template (or pattern), cut in cardboard or grease-proof paper, is used for marking accurately a design on the top or sides of the cake. Once templates have been accurately measured to fit your tins, they may be stored for future use. Label and mark suitably.

3. Use cotton balls or cotton wool to prop up petals while they dry or when arranging them on a cake.

4. Uncooked fruit cake mixture (well sealed) may be kept in a freezer for up to six months. Defrost at room temperature and bake as usual.

5. Lay a sheet of plastic foam on the table when arranging flowers on a cake. It prevents breakage if one is dropped. Also a small piece of foam placed on the bottom of the delivery carton prevents movement and vibration.

6. It is better to under-decorate than over-decorate.

7. Insert wires into icing only; some wire has a copper filament in the centre and this should not touch the cake itself.

8. For small quantities of royal icing it is not necessary to mix a whole egg white; use a teaspoon of egg white, adding pure icing sugar and mix to the required consistency.

9. Mould the centres for daisies and pea flowers at least 24 hours before use.

10. Sieve pure icing sugar through muslin or a clean piece of nylon stocking.

11. Prepare wires (cut and hooked or knotted), water, maize cornflour and tools before commencing to mould. Maize cornflour is very fine and soft, whereas wheat cornflour is much coarser and could scratch fine petals.

12. When pricing cakes include every small item: glue, board, egg whites, cake, marzipan, fondants, royal icing, ribbon and wire, pillars and paper — plus your estimate of time.

13. When experimenting with a new flower, have a fresh flower or a good colour photograph in front of you for reference.

14. Excessively humid or wet weather alters consistency, so at such times the decorator should try to work in the cool of the day.

15. Under extreme conditions, a *very little* more icing sugar may be added to covering fondant to gain correct consistency—but no more than the maximum stated in recipe, or it will set too hard.

16. Care must be taken when measuring water and glucose; too much of either makes modelling and covering fondants too soft.

17. Gelatine must always be completely dissolved. If one grain is not dissolved a mould will form in the modelling fondant. Correct consistency of modelling fondant is of prime importance for moulded flowers.

18. All spoon measurements given are level.

19. If cutting butter cakes to a fancy shape, place them in the freezer until very firm but not frozen. They can then be trimmed with an electric knife (or a very sharp knife) and will not crumble or tear.

20. Left-over cottons from stamens, dipped in pale colours and then in gelatine, make stamens for small flowers. A spot of nail polish gives them a pearl lustre. Or dip stamen cottons into royal icing thinned with egg white for tiny stamens.

21. A general rule: add colour with care—you can always add more, but you can't take it out.

22. Tint stamens by dipping a small bundle into pastel coloured methylated spirits—dip the bundle in quickly, spread to dry on a tissue. They may be dipped again if not deep enough in colour.

23. If you have excessively perspiring hands use a pair of disposable plastic gloves when mixing all fondants—and also when shaping petals, etc.

Two-tier cream coloured wedding cake with golden single roses,
mauve hyacinths, simple embossed rose embroidery, tiny bluebirds
and lace.

16
RECIPES

Boiled Almond Paste

This is a rich almond paste, used only on very special cakes. A confectionery thermometer is used in this recipe.

1 kg (2 lb) crystal sugar
150 g (5 oz) glucose
1 cup water
680 g (1½ lb) ground almonds
4 tablespoons rum
1 egg
4 egg yolks
1 kg (2 lb) pure icing sugar (*sifted*)

Combine the ingredients in a saucepan, stir until sugar dissolves, add confectionery thermometer, then boil to 110°C (235°F). Allow to cool slightly, then add ground almonds, rum, egg and egg yolks. Mix well and add pure icing sugar, kneading well.

Toffee Glaze for Marzipan Fruit

This glaze can become sticky and soft in very humid weather, so it's best to apply coating the day it is required.

¼ cup water
½ cup crystal sugar
pinch of cream of tartar

Place ingredients in a saucepan and stir gently over moderate heat until the sugar has dissolved. Increase the heat and boil rapidly (without stirring) until the mixture changes to light golden. (Have a greased cake cooler ready.) Remove the glaze from the heat, place fruit one at a time on a fine-pronged fork and dip quickly into the glaze to obtain a thin coating. Place on cooler to set.

Covering Fondant 2

2 egg whites
1 kg (2 lb) pure icing sugar
125 g (4 oz) liquid glucose or light corn syrup
2 teaspoons glycerine
colouring and flavouring (*optional*)

Sift icing sugar into a glass bowl, make a well in the centre and add glucose (softened if necessary over hot water) and lightly beaten egg whites. Mix the ingredients well with a wooden spoon, then add the sifted icing sugar a little at a time, until the mixture is a stiff paste. Turn out onto a board that has been dusted with sifted icing sugar, and knead until smooth. Add colouring and flavouring if desired.

When the correct consistency is obtained, an impression of the finger should be maintained when the icing is squeezed and there should be no stickiness left on the fingers.

Note: Leftover fondant can be flavoured and set in small confectionery moulds. Dip in chocolate if desired. Children love them.

Supreme Plastic Fondant

A confectionery thermometer is required to make this excellent fondant covering. Make it at least one day before it is required.

Group A

⅔ cup (5 oz) water
125 g (4 oz) liquid glucose
500 g (1 lb) crystal sugar
30 ml (1 oz) glycerine
1 teaspoon cream of tartar

Group B

⅔ cup water (5 oz)
30 g (1 oz) gelatine
125 g (4 oz) copha
2.25 kg (4½ lb) pure icing sugar (sifted)

Boil Group A to 120°C (240°F) or soft-ball consistency when tested in cold water. Remove from heat and allow bubbles to subside. Dissolve gelatine in ⅔ cup water, add to mixture; add chopped copha and allow to cool. Beat in half the pure icing sugar gradually. Place in a sealed plastic container and leave for not less than 24 hours, or until required. Before using, knead in the balance of the sifted icing sugar until a plastic consistency is obtained. This mixture will cover a large two-tier cake, a small three-tier cake, or three single 250 g (½ lb) cakes.

Warm Icing

250 g (8 oz) pure icing sugar (*sifted*)
good squeeze of lemon or orange juice
1 teaspoon butter

Place the cake on a prepared board or plate. Prepare a collar, a double thickness of waxed paper about 25 mm (1 in) wide, place around the top of the cake so paper

Basket cake piped with royal icing and filled with flowers including
pansies, roses, heather, daffodils, flannel flowers and jasmine.

is 6 mm (¼ in) above top of cake, and secure with a pin.

Mix icing sugar and lemon juice to a firm consistency, add butter and place on low heat, stirring with wooden spoon till butter melts. While warm, pour evenly over the top of the cake. Allow to stand until set.

Butter Icing

125 g (4 oz) butter
250 g (8 oz) pure icing sugar (*sifted*)
2 tablespoons sherry, lemon or orange juice

Cream butter and icing sugar, add liquid and beat until smooth. Spread evenly on the cake with a knife or spatula that has been dipped into milk. Vienna icing is made by the addition to this of 2 tablespoons of sifted cocoa.

Large Rich Butter Cake

On occasions people ask for a large butter cake, instead of a fruit cake. This mixture will fill a 185 mm (9 in) square tin, 80 mm (3 in) deep. It is firm enough to take a thin marzipan covering and fondant covering 6 mm (¼ in) thick.

375 g (¾ lb) butter
2 cups caster sugar
2 teaspoons vanilla essence
7 eggs
6 cups self-raising flour
1 cup (approx) milk

Cream butter and sugar, add vanilla, eggs (one at a time), beating well after each addition so the mixture does not curdle. Add milk and flour alternately in small quantities, mixing thoroughly. Pour into a well greased tin. Bake in a moderate oven for about 1½ hours, until golden brown on top. Cool in the tin.

Génoise Cake

60 g (2½ oz) self-raising flour
1 tablespoon (2½ oz) cornflour
3 eggs
125 g (4 oz) sugar
100 g (3 oz) butter or margarine, melted

Sift flour and cornflour. Place eggs and sugar in a basin over warm water and whisk lightly until the mixture is stiff enough to retain the impression of the whisk for a few seconds. Remove the basin from heat. Sift half the flour mixture over the surface and fold in *very lightly*. Add balance of flour in the same way, alternately with melted butter. Pour into greased and lined slab tin. Bake in a moderate oven until golden brown (about 45 minutes, depending on depth of tin).

Note: This recipe is suitable for cutting into fancy shapes for petits fours, rose cakes and so on. For best results allow the cake to stand for 24 hours before cutting. If this is not possible place it in the freezer for a short time until firm, but not frozen, then it will cut without crumbling.

Rose Cakes

Rose cakes are made from Génoise mixture. Cut shapes with a small scone cutter, then coat the sides with jam, toasted coconut or crushed nuts. Decorate the top with petals moulded from coloured marzipan in the shape of an open rose. Chopped nuts or a glacé cherry form the centre.

Children's Party Cakes

Genoise mixture may also be baked in wafer icecream cups. When cool, cover tops with chocolate icing and decorate with hundreds and thousands, jelly beans or other small sweets.

Marble Cake

This cake is suitable for using as the base of a Dolly Varden cake, the colours in the cake being one of the main attractions for children. It is baked in a special Dolly Varden tin, shaped rather like a basin. This quantity fits a larger size tin.

250 g (½ lb) butter
250 g (½ lb) sugar
3 eggs
⅓ cup milk
vanilla essence
375 g (12 oz) self-raising flour
few drops red colouring
2 tablespoons cocoa (*sifted*)

Grease and line the tin. Cream butter and sugar, add well beaten eggs, mixing well. Add milk and vanilla, then sifted flour. Divide the mixture into three equal parts; leave one part plain, colour one pink, add cocoa to the third. Place alternate spoonfuls in the tin. Bake in a moderate oven for about 1 hour.

Note: The Dolly Varden tin can also be used for other cakes, such as clown's head (photo page 84), Father Christmas face, Christmas tree, and Indian teepee.

Individual clown cakes for a children's party can be made in small basins.

Rich Fruit Cake

This quantity will fill a 200 mm (8 in) square tin; halve the mixture for 150 mm (6 in) tin; double it for 250 mm (10 in) tin.

250 g (8 oz) each currants, sultanas and raisins
90 g (3 oz) each dates and prunes
60 g (2 oz) each mixed peel and glacé cherries (*optional extras* apricots, figs)
60 g (2 oz) almonds
2 tablespoons each rum, brandy and sherry
5 eggs
250 g (8 oz) butter
250 g (8 oz) brown sugar
300 g (10 oz) plain flour
1 teaspoon each nutmeg, cinnamon, mixed spice

Fluids — all in one dish

1 tablespoon plum jam
1 teaspoon vanilla essence
1 teaspoon Parisienne essence
2 tablespoons golden syrup
1 teaspoon glycerine
1 tablespoon lemon essence

Cut fruit and soak in alcohol. Leave for at least 24 hours to blend. Cream butter and sugar, add eggs one at a time, beating thoroughly after each addition. Add fluids, then sifted dry ingredients and fruit alternately, mixing well. Place into a lined cake tin and smooth the top with a spatula that has been dipped in water. To release air pockets, drop the tin several times from just above bench. Place tin low in the oven and bake at 120°C (275°F) for 3-3½ hours. When cooked, while still hot, pour 2 tablespoons of extra sherry over the cake. Allow to cool in tin, then wrap in foil and a towel for 6 weeks to mature.

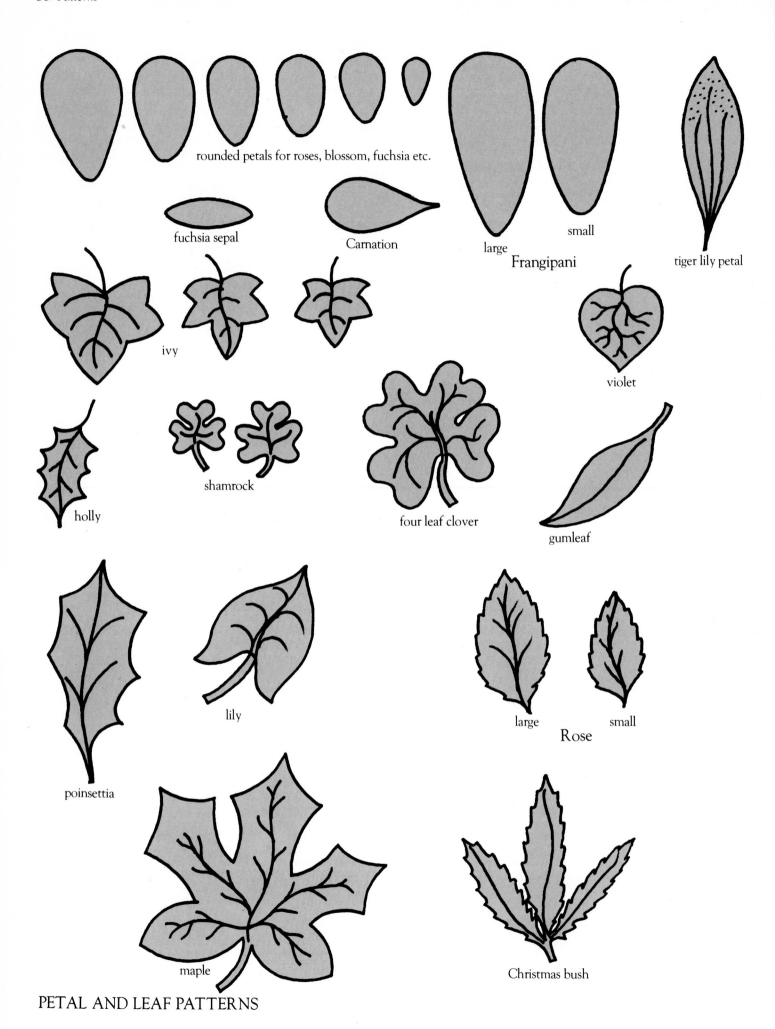

rounded petals for roses, blossom, fuchsia etc.

fuchsia sepal

Carnation

large   small
Frangipani

tiger lily petal

ivy

violet

holly

shamrock

four leaf clover

gumleaf

poinsettia

lily

large   small
Rose

maple

Christmas bush

PETAL AND LEAF PATTERNS

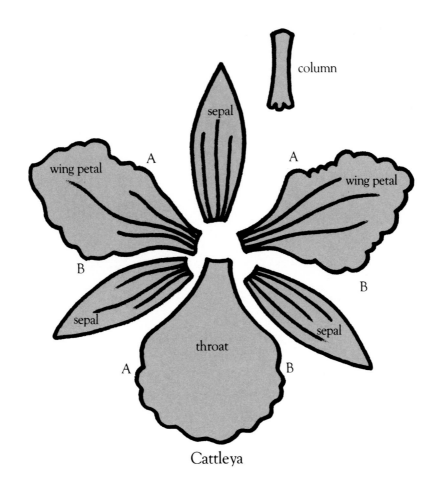

Cattleya

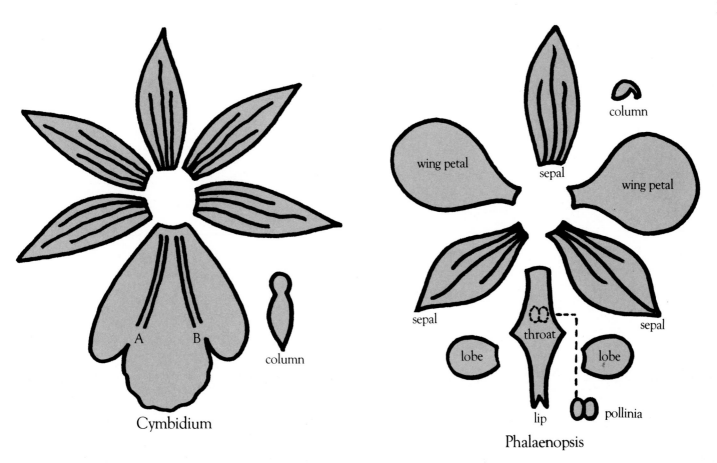

Cymbidium

Phalaenopsis

ORCHID PATTERNS

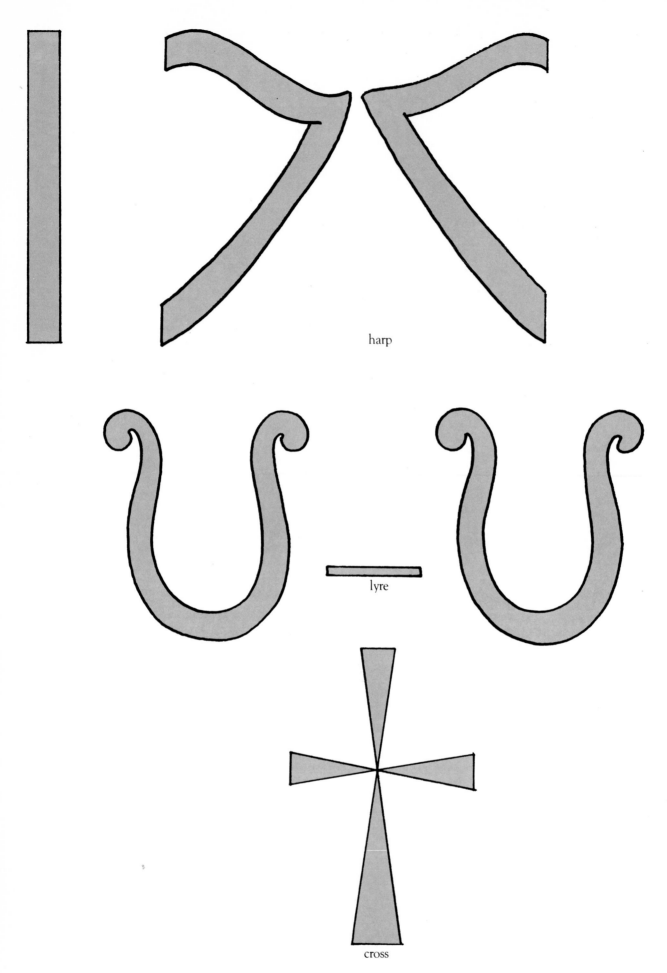

harp

lyre

cross

PATTERNS FOR ORNAMENTS

horseshoes

keys

shield for coat of arms

stars

PATTERNS FOR ORNAMENTS

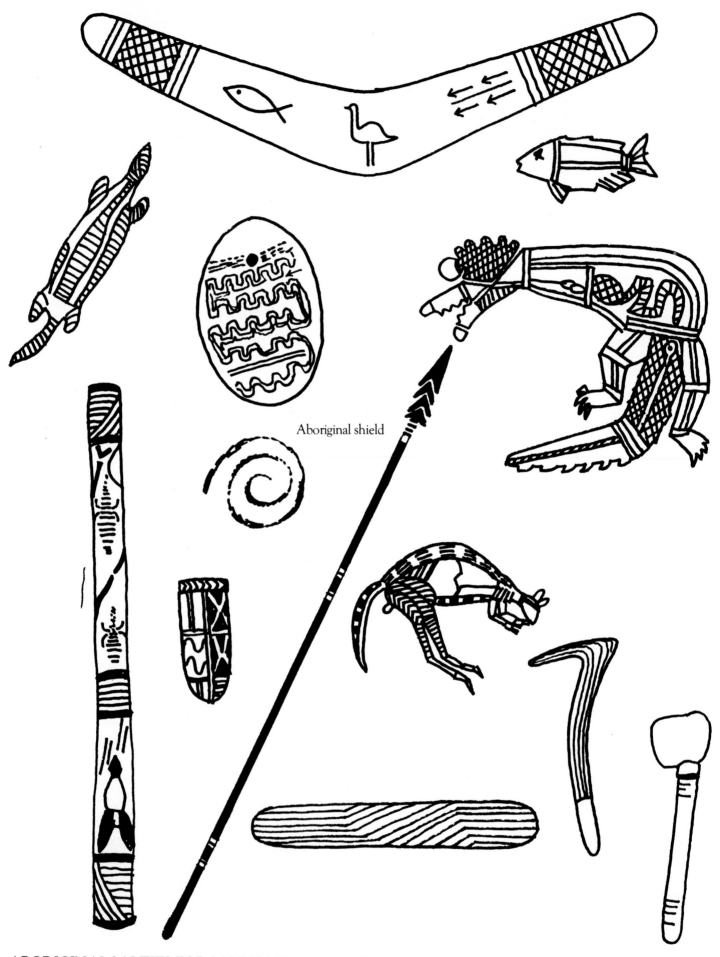

Aboriginal shield

ABORIGINAL MOTIFS FOR MODELLING AND PIPING

Father Christmas

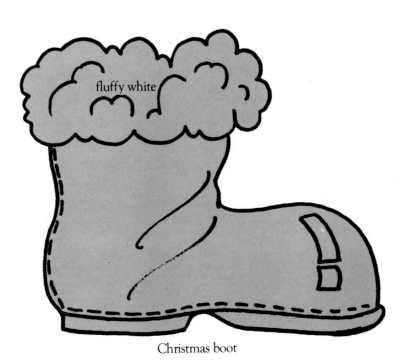

fluffy white

Christmas boot

DESIGNS FOR FLOODING OR PAINTING

baby's bib
decorate plaque as desired

DESIGNS FOR FLOODING OR PAINTING

DESIGNS FOR FLOODING OR PAINTING

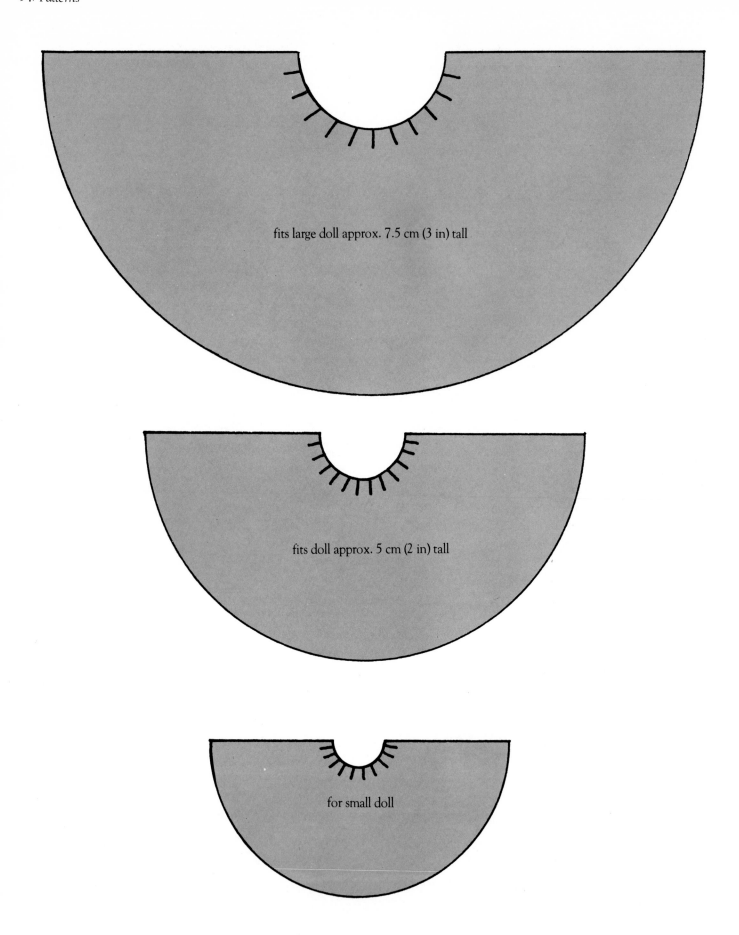

fits large doll approx. 7.5 cm (3 in) tall

fits doll approx. 5 cm (2 in) tall

for small doll

DOLLS' SKIRT PATTERNS

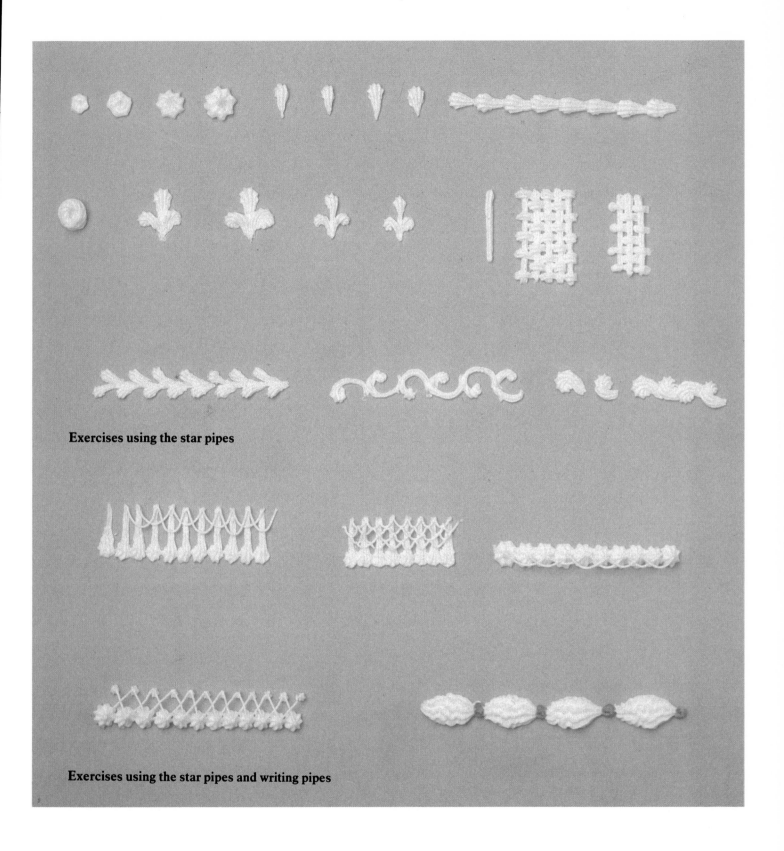

Exercises using the star pipes

Exercises using the star pipes and writing pipes

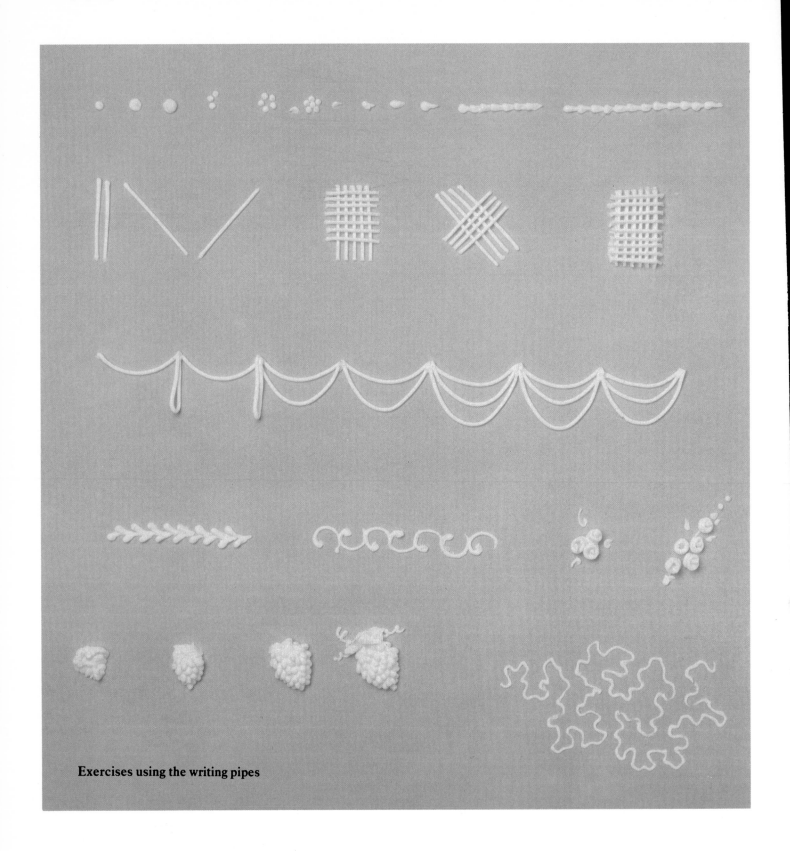

Exercises using the writing pipes

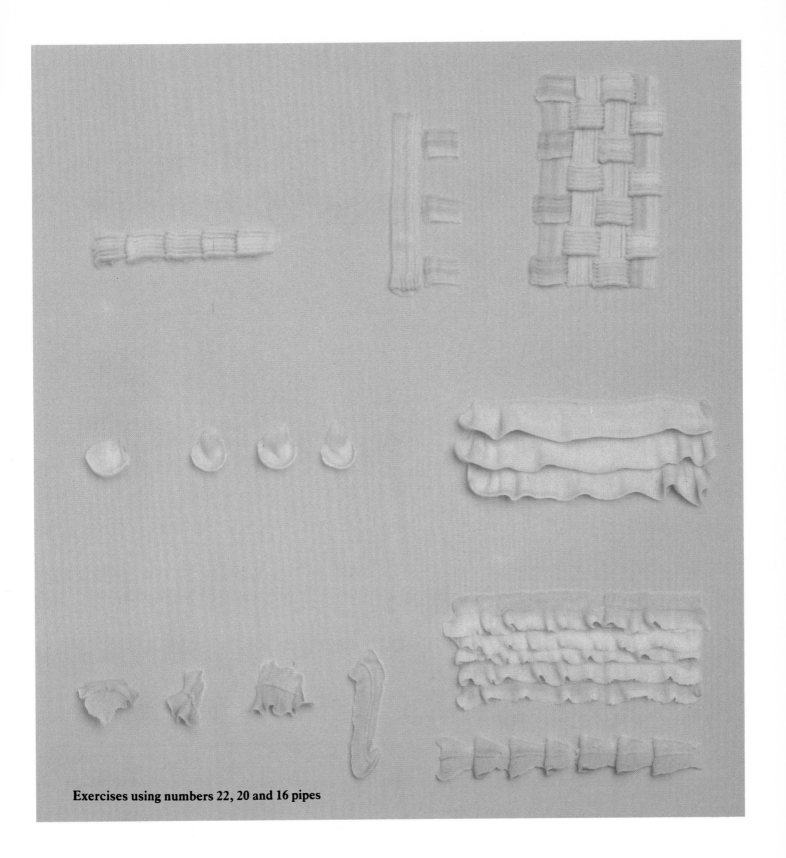

Exercises using numbers 22, 20 and 16 pipes

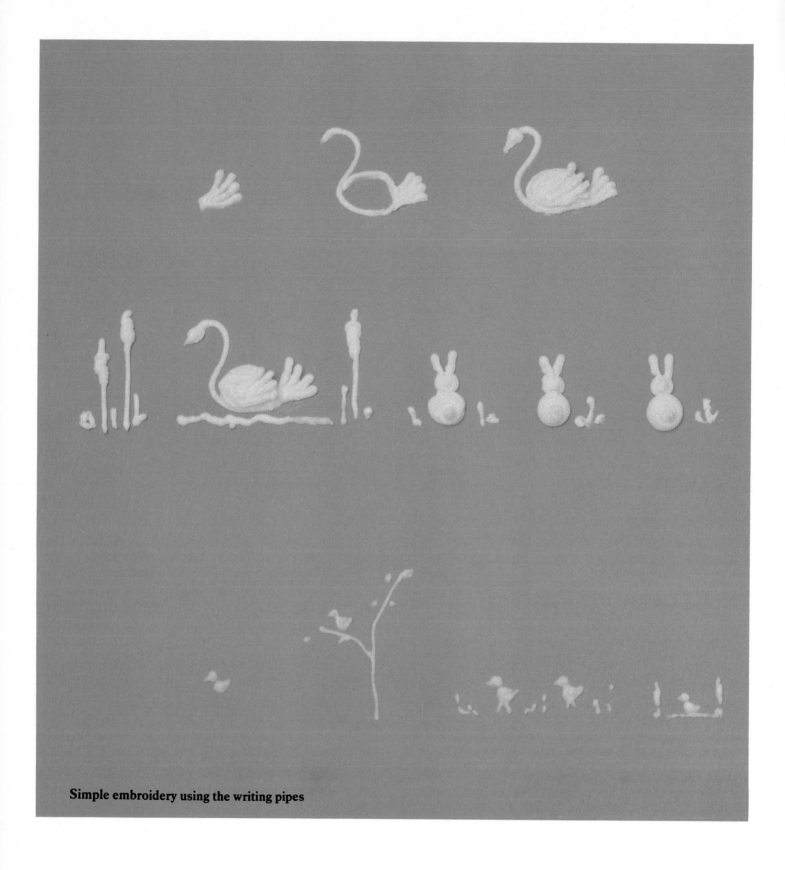

Simple embroidery using the writing pipes

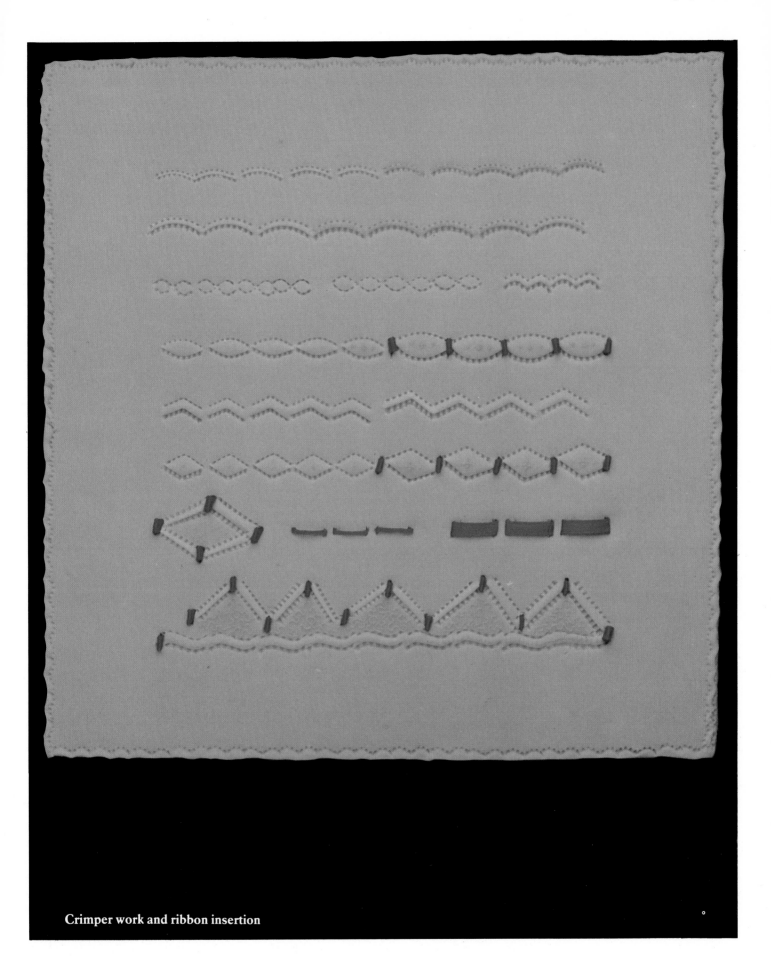

Crimper work and ribbon insertion

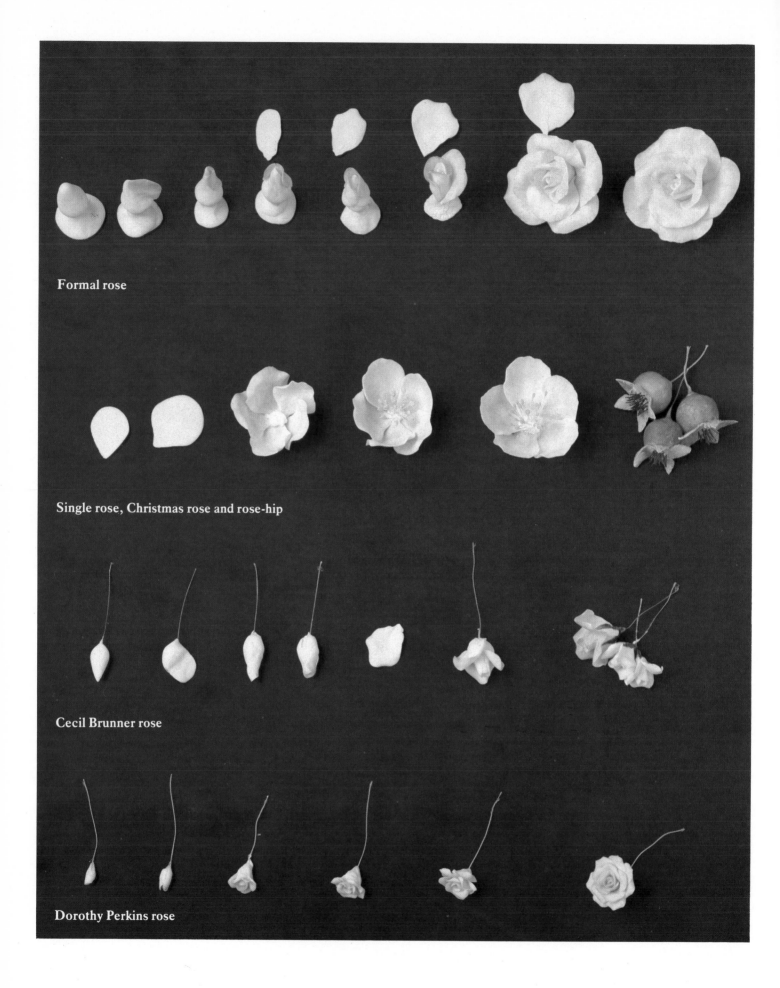

Formal rose

Single rose, Christmas rose and rose-hip

Cecil Brunner rose

Dorothy Perkins rose

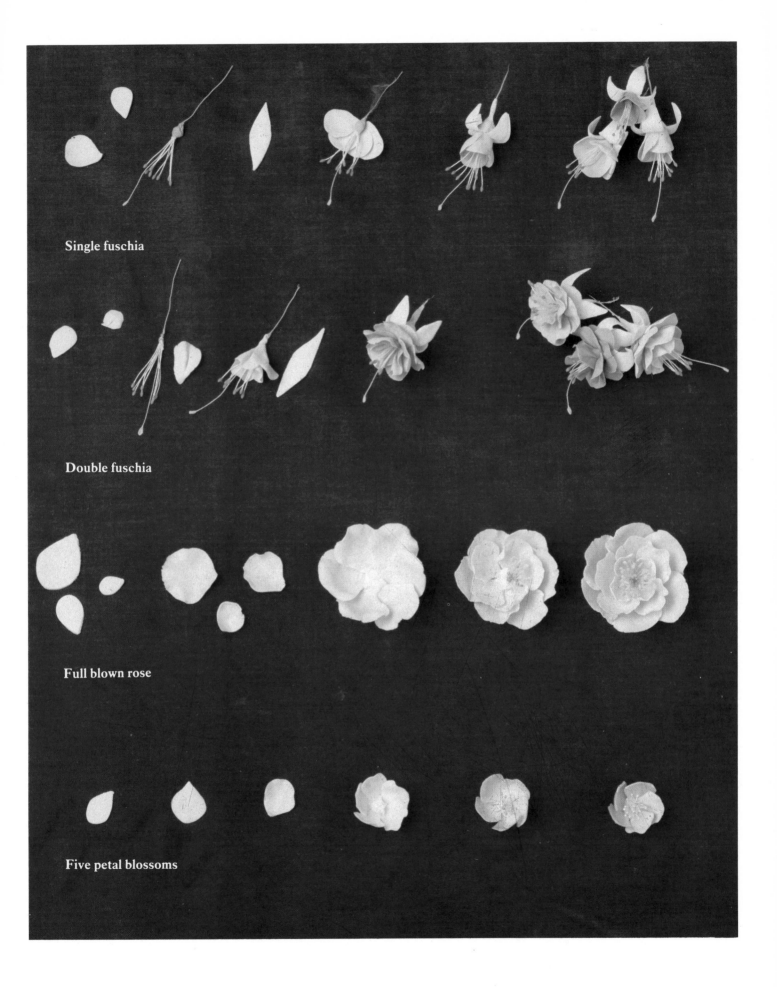

Single fuschia

Double fuschia

Full blown rose

Five petal blossoms

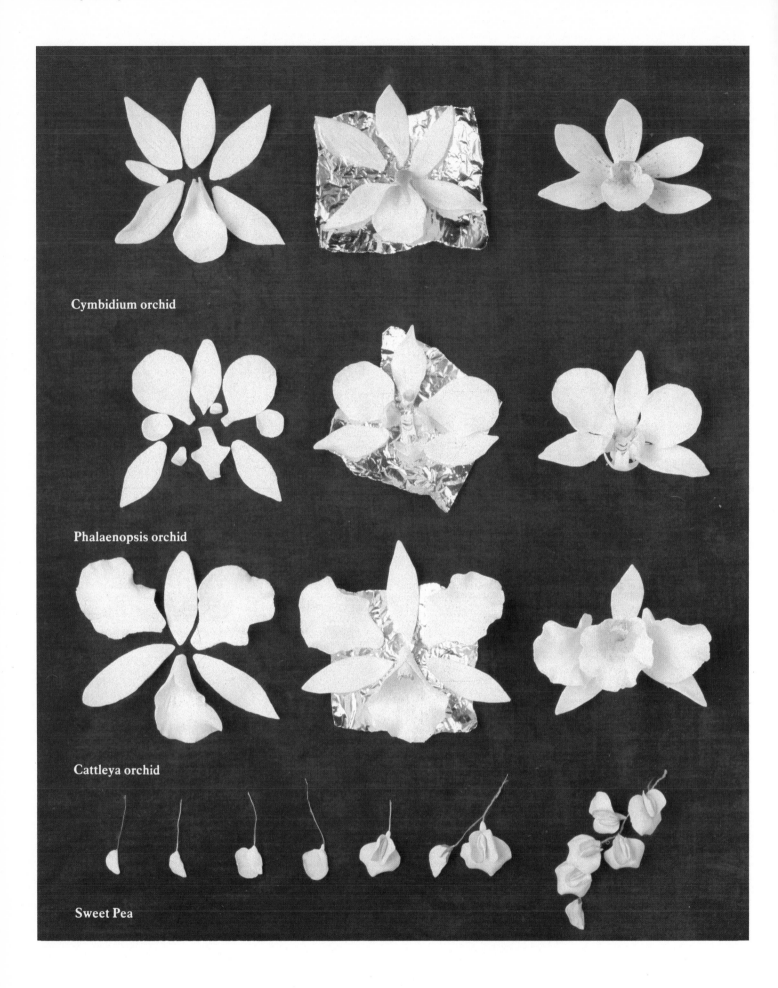

Cymbidium orchid

Phalaenopsis orchid

Cattleya orchid

Sweet Pea

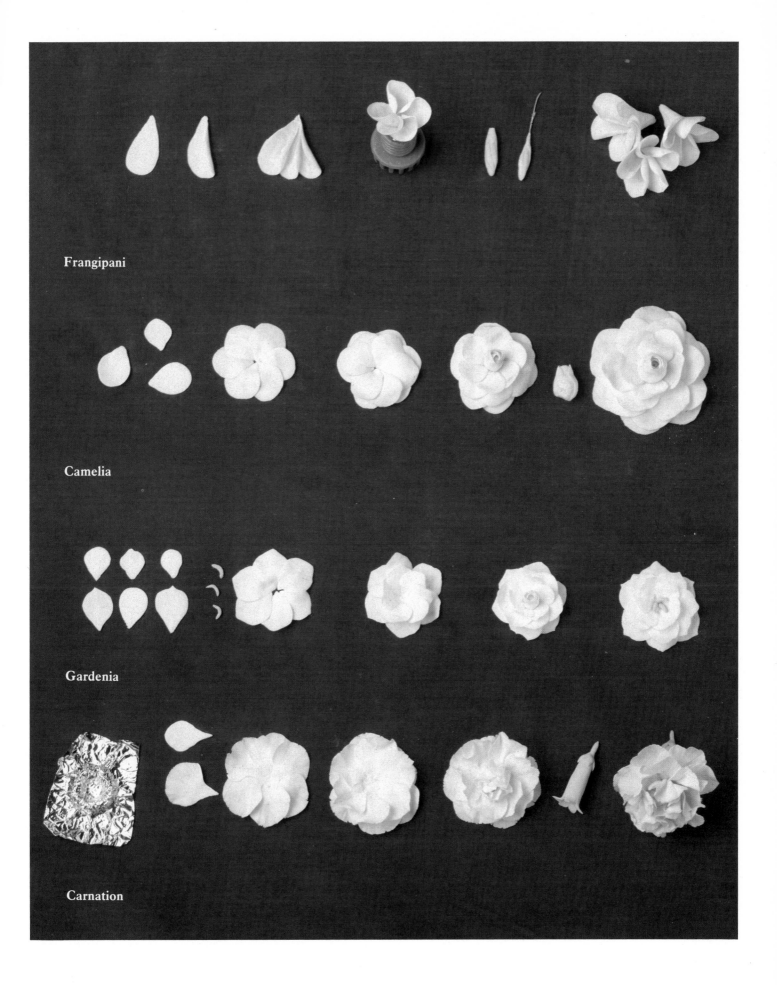

Frangipani

Camelia

Gardenia

Carnation

Tiger Lily

Waratah   **Method 1**   **Method 2**

Daisies

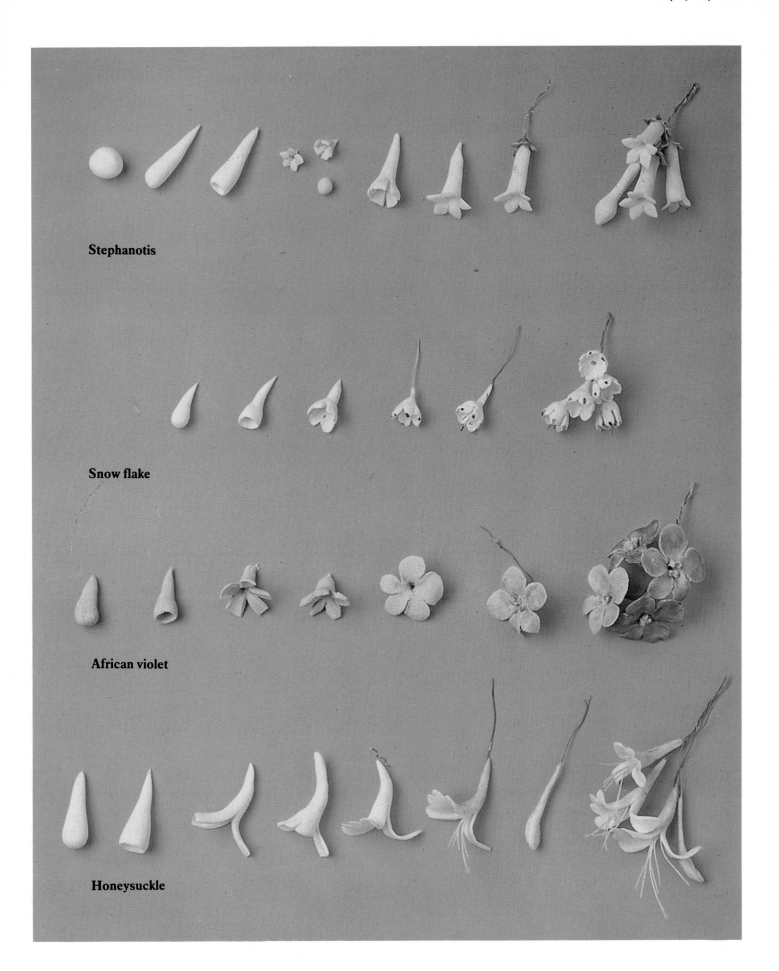

Stephanotis

Snow flake

African violet

Honeysuckle

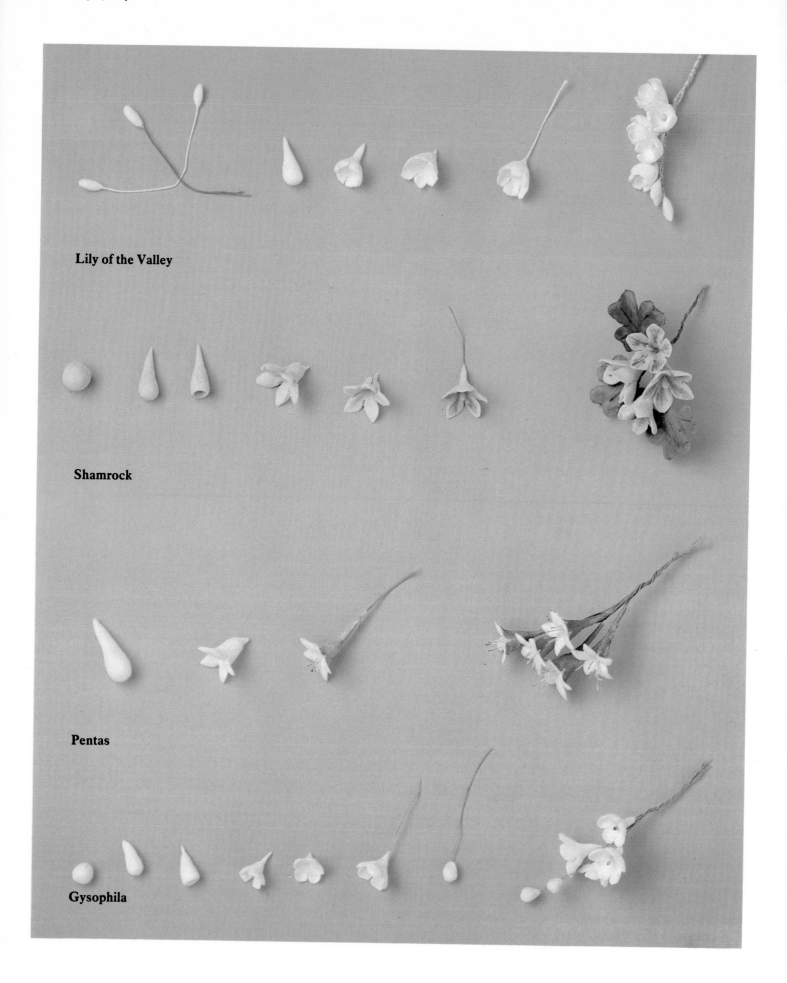

Lily of the Valley

Shamrock

Pentas

Gysophila

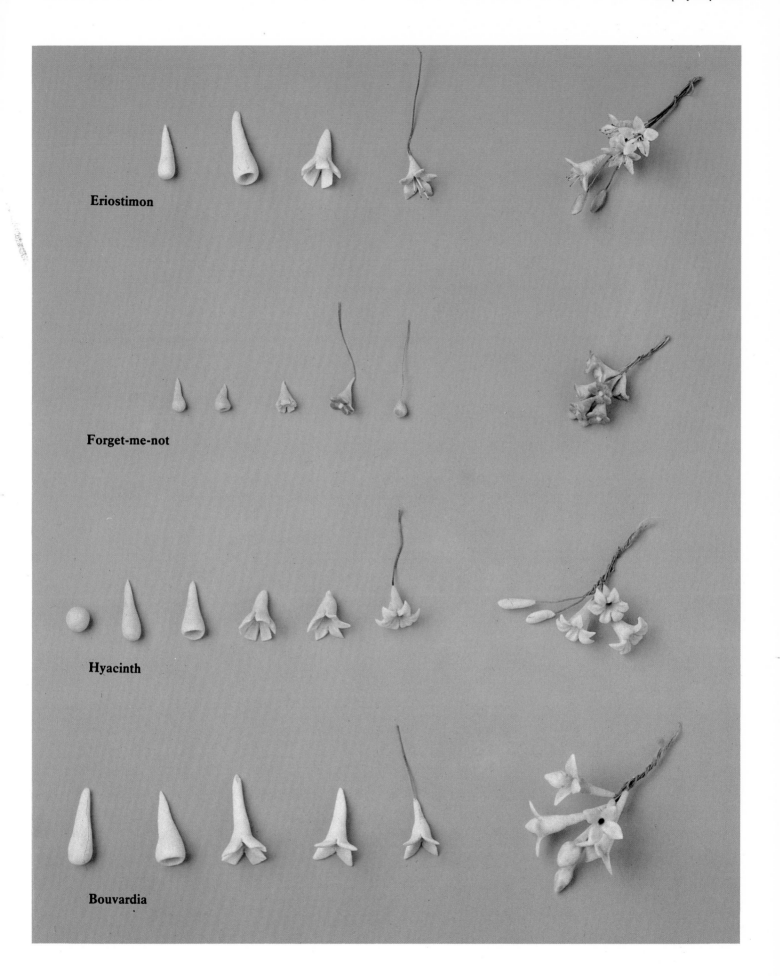

Eriostimon

Forget-me-not

Hyacinth

Bouvardia

Christmas decorations

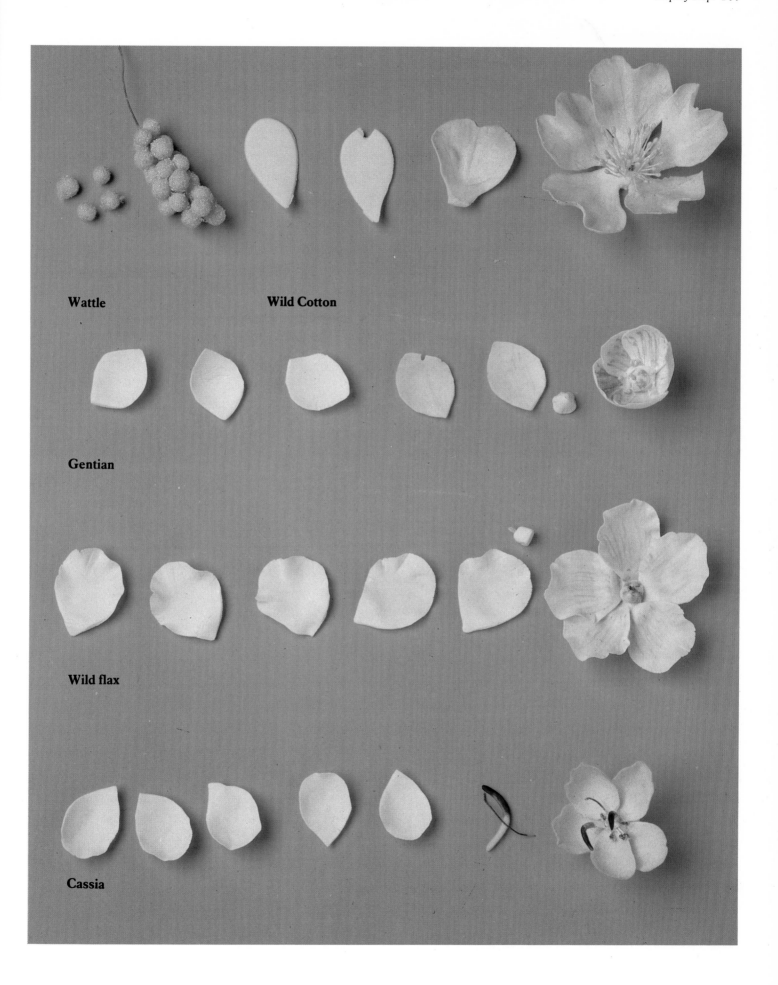

Wattle

Wild Cotton

Gentian

Wild flax

Cassia

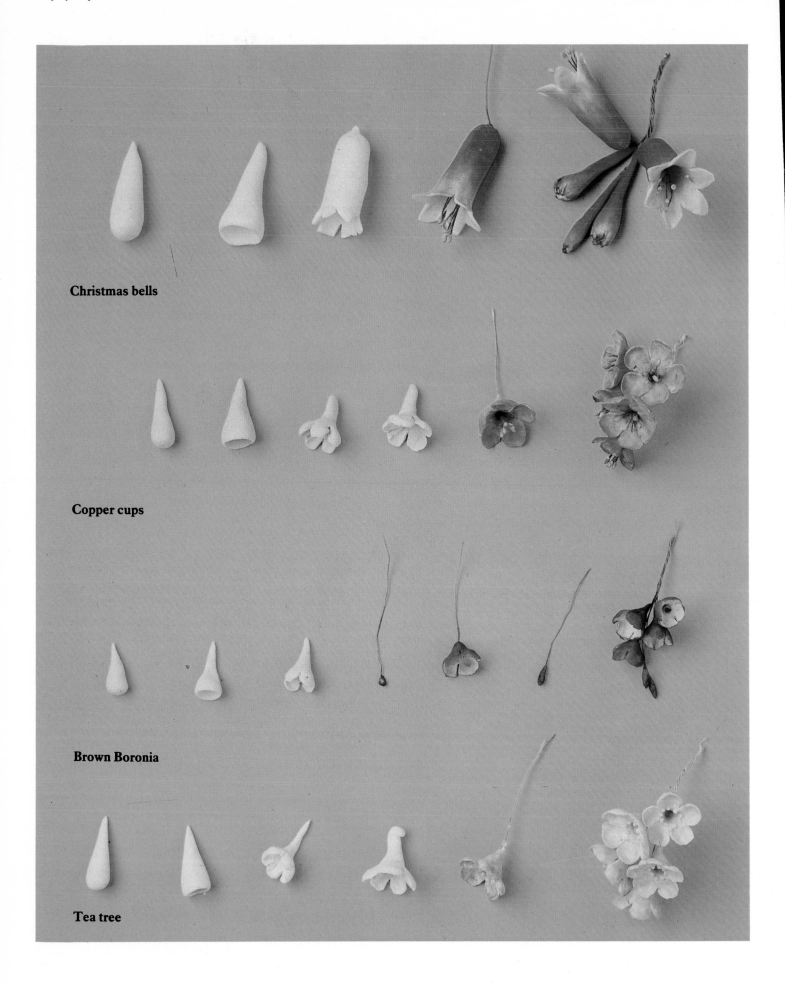

Christmas bells

Copper cups

Brown Boronia

Tea tree

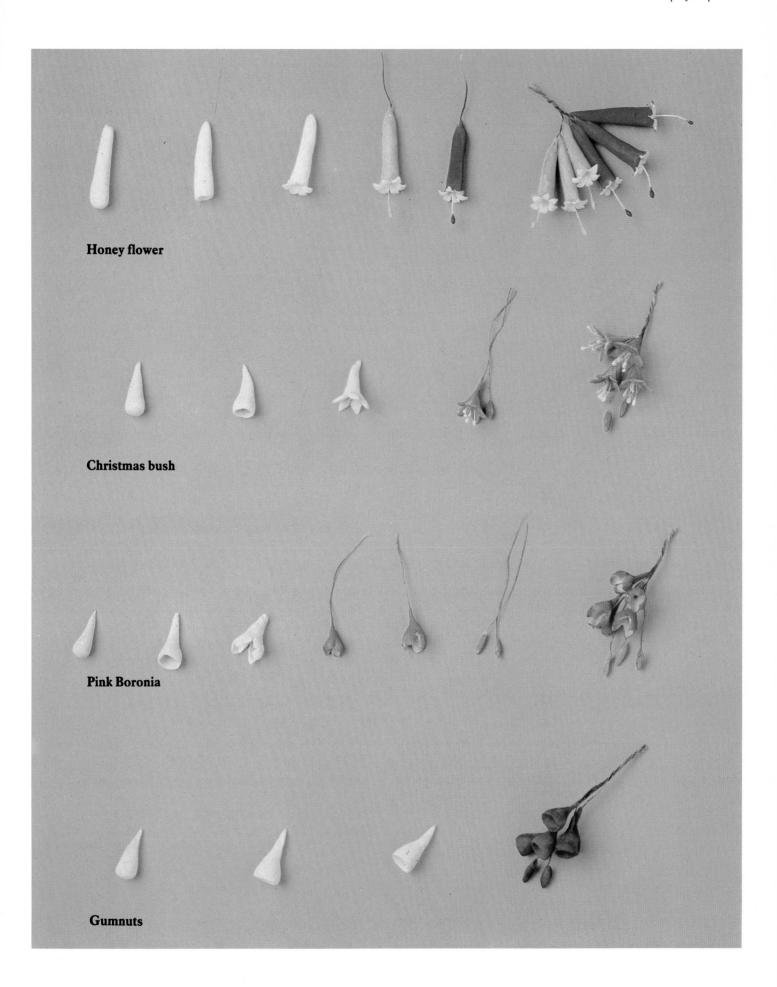

Honey flower

Christmas bush

Pink Boronia

Gumnuts

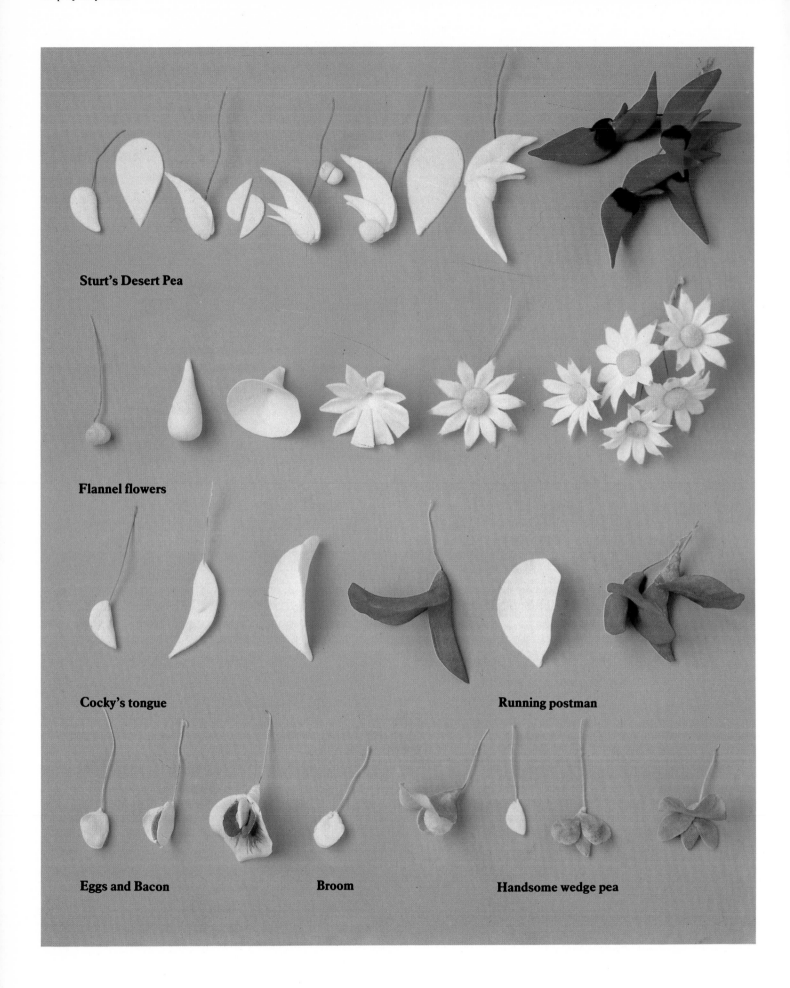

Sturt's Desert Pea

Flannel flowers

Cocky's tongue

Running postman

Eggs and Bacon

Broom

Handsome wedge pea

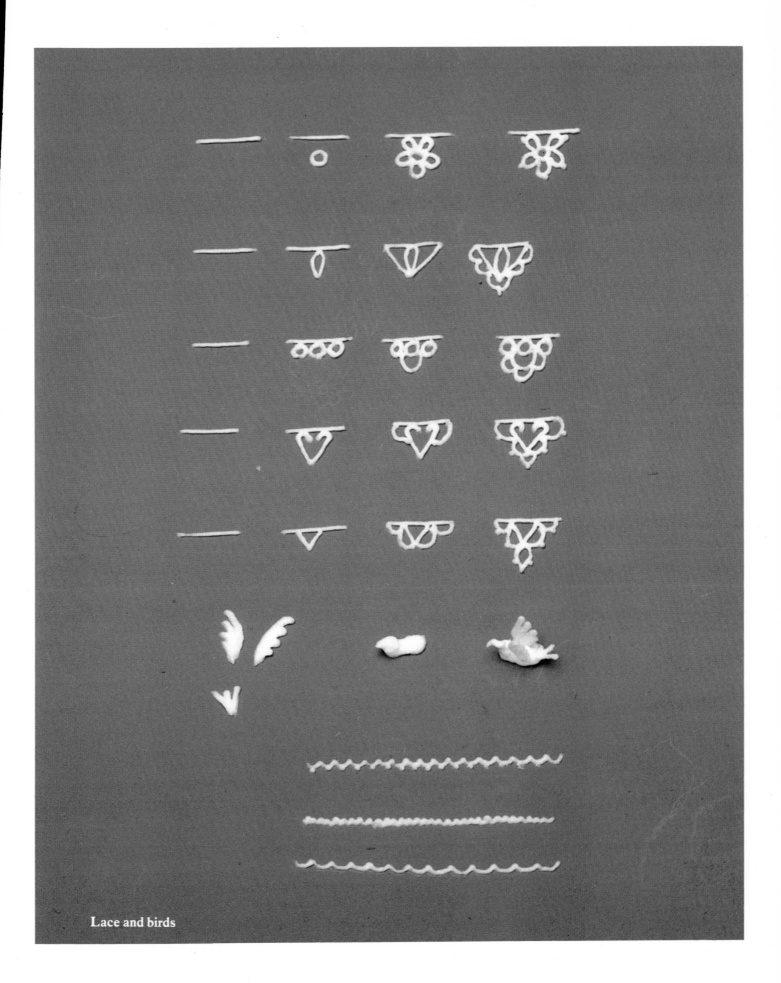

Lace and birds

Marzipans

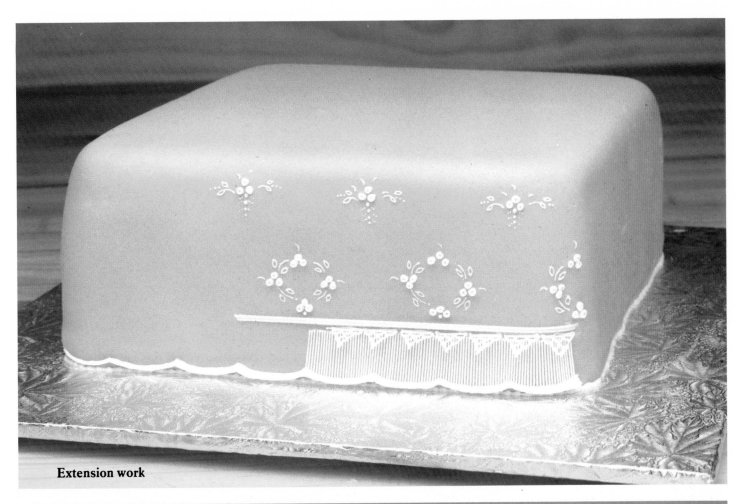

Extension work

Embroidery

Piped flowers

Piped flowers

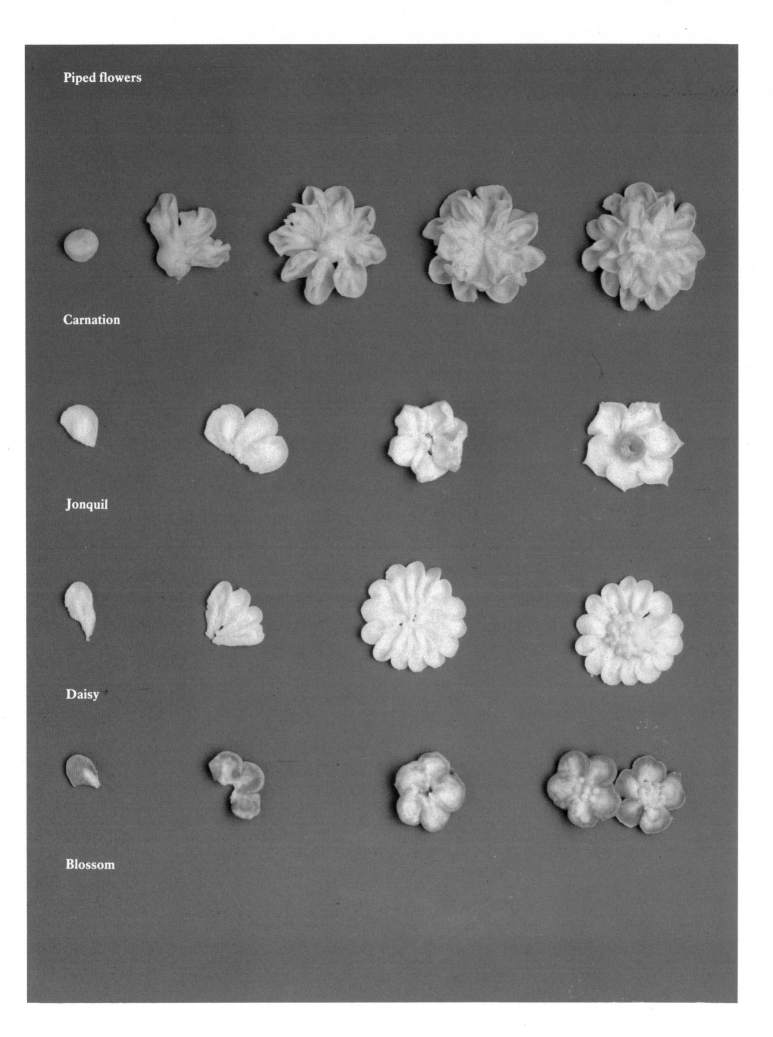

Carnation

Jonquil

Daisy

Blossom

Piped flowers

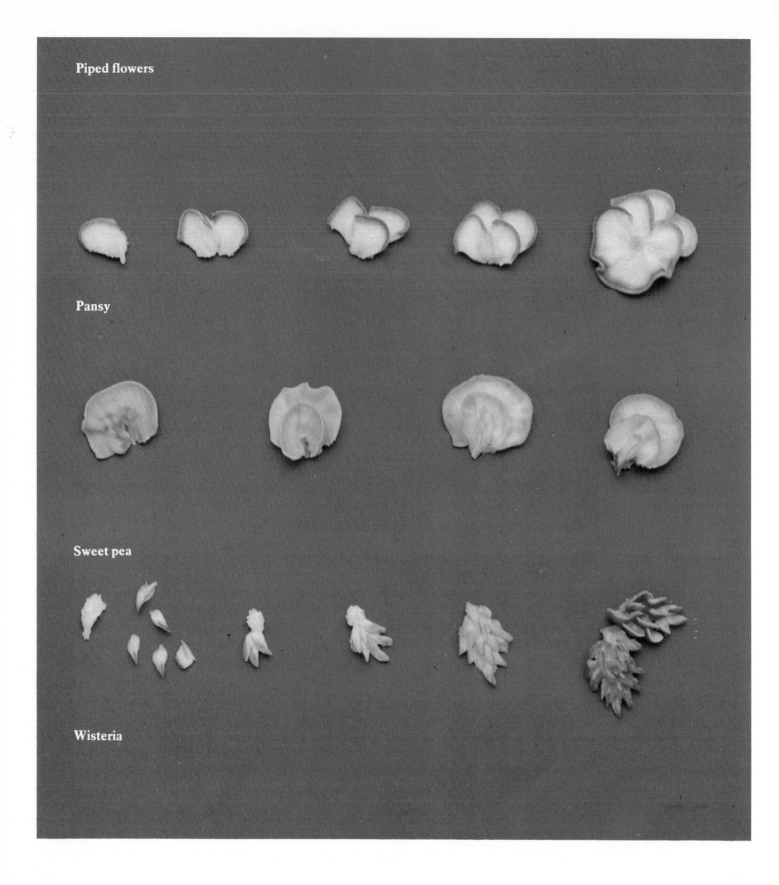

Pansy

Sweet pea

Wisteria

INDEX